A Second Later, Kellogg Heard the Arrows.

Whit, whit, whit. He saw them streak past. *Whit-tuk!* *S-thung!* He felt the pain like a red-hot iron bar driving into his back. He stood rooted in his tracks for a moment, reaching desperately for the arrow. His hand came away stained with blood.

Pain burned up into his shoulders and neck, then numbed; he dropped down and began crawling again. He must reach Custer's headquarters position. Kellogg crawled until his hands and knees were raw. How much of luck there is in life, he thought. A whim of chance had brought him to this field of death. His fingers touched the wide leather belt around his waist. Clem Lounsberry's belt, lucky talisman. "My Civil War Belt," Lounsberry had said proudly. "Take it for luck, Mark. It saved my life once. See the old bloodstain on it."

There would be plenty of blood on Lounsberry's belt this time, he thought.

Other books by Dee Brown available from Dell

QUANTITY SALES

Most Dell books are available at special quantity discounts when purchased in bulk by corporations, organizations, and special-interest groups. Custom imprinting or excerpting can also be done to fit special needs. For details write: Dell Publishing, 666 Fifth Avenue, New York, NY 10103. Attn.: Special Sales Department.

INDIVIDUAL SALES

Are there any Dell books you want but cannot find in your local stores? If so, you can order them directly from us. You can get any Dell book in print. Simply include the book's title, author, and ISBN number if you have it, along with a check or money order (no cash can be accepted) for the full retail price plus $1.50 to cover shipping and handling. Mail to: Dell Readers Service, P.O. Box 5057, Des Plaines, IL 60017.

Showdown at Little Big Horn

Dee Brown

A DELL BOOK

Published by
Dell Publishing
a division of
The Bantam Doubleday Dell
Publishing Group, Inc.
666 Fifth Avenue
New York, New York 10103

ISBN: 0-440-20202-7

Printed in the United States of America
Published simultaneously in Canada

October 1988

10 9 8 7 6 5 4 3 2 1

KRI

Contents

1

Mark Kellogg

May 11, 1876

A cold splash of rain struck Mark Kellogg's face when he stepped out of his boardinghouse. He drew his buffalo coat tight around his chest, looped it, and hurried along the wooden sidewalk, head down against the wind. In less than five minutes he was standing under a swaying sign: BIS-MARCK TRIBUNE. C. A. LOUNSBERRY, EDITOR AND PROPRIETOR. He inserted a key in the door and entered a one-room print shop and editorial office.

Kellogg opened the draft on the potbellied stove and tossed in a shovelful of coal. He removed his damp coat, and then walked to a desk and lighted an overhead oil lamp to relieve the gloom. Through the rain-streaked window he saw a team of mules pulling an army ambulance slowly along the muddy street. He watched until it passed from view, then casually reached out and turned the leaf of his calendar to May 11, 1876.

In another week, he thought, Custer should be leading his men out on the Big Horn expedition. From all the talk going around, this summer should see a showdown between the hostile tribes and the Army. For weeks, Sioux and Cheyennes had been leaving their reservations in droves. Almost every day, scouts brought in rumors of the mightiest concentration of warriors ever assembled back in the Powder River country. Sitting Bull and Crazy Horse were boasting that this time they would rub out all the bluecoat soldiers and take back their hunting grounds forever.

Kellogg peered out at the gray rain mist obscuring the Missouri River. Across the river lay Fort Abraham Lincoln, and there the 7th Cavalry awaited orders to march. The young printer-editor could not help but envy the good fortune of his friend and employer, Clement Lounsberry. A few days earlier, Lounsberry had received a telegram from New York appointing him official correspondent of the New York *Herald* for the Indian expedition.

At the time, Kellogg had expressed his congratulations. "That's a real feather in your cap, Clem," he had said.

"I suppose so," Lounsberry replied, "but it'll mean a busy summer for you, getting out this paper by yourself."

Kellogg had mumbled something in reply. He would have given almost anything to be in Lounsberry's place.

Standing now at the window overlooking the deserted street, he saw Lounsberry turn the nearest corner and come hurrying through the pelting rain. A moment later the front door swung inward.

"Good morning," Kellogg said, and then took a second look at his friend. "Why so glum this morning, Clem?"

Lounsberry shook his head, his face still serious. "Something's come up, Mark. Everything's changed."

Kellogg could read the disappointment in his friend's eyes. "What's wrong?"

"My wife has been ill, you know, and begging me not to go on the Indian expedition. I thought I'd convinced her I'd be safe with General Custer, but last night I talked with Custer and he advised me to find a replacement."

Kellogg frowned. "Will it be that dangerous?"

"No. What it boils down to is that I have two good reasons not to go—my wife's health, and the fact that I'm too well known as a newspaperman. You see, General Sherman has forbidden Custer to take along any newspaper correspondents."

Kellogg stared in disbelief. "I don't understand."

Lounsberry shrugged. "It's all part of the political stew Custer stumbled into when he exposed those thieving Indian Bureau officials. First, he was told he could not go on the expedition. Then he was told he could lead the 7th Cavalry but General Terry will be in command of field operations and will give all the orders. Now they forbid him to take official newspaper correspondents. That's where you come in, Mark."

Kellogg's eyes widened. "How so?"

"Custer would like to have you along as his personal guest. You're not an accredited correspondent, but nothing's to stop you from keeping a daily journal. The expedition will be sending couriers back to Fort Lincoln regularly, and Custer will see that your reports reach me by those runners. What I do with them is my business, but I'm rather sure the New York *Herald* and other newspapers will receive your stories."

Kellogg chuckled softly. "You can't beat Custer. He understands the power of the press, all right."

"Newspapers made Custer a national hero, and he knows it. He'd like to keep on being a hero. Sometimes I suspect he'd like to run for President." Lounsberry gave his friend a sharp glance. "Are you game for it, Mark?"

"Of course I am. I wouldn't miss it." Kellogg gripped Lounsberry's hand. "What do I do first?"

"Get over to Fort Lincoln on the next ferryboat and see Custer. He'll be expecting you."

By the time Kellogg reached the ferry landing, the rain had stopped and the gray cloud masses were breaking up, exposing faint patches of blue. When he stepped onto the battered deck of the boat, he noticed a familiar figure lounging beside an army ambulance which had just drawn aboard. "Dr. DeWolf!" Kellogg cried cordially. "What brought you to our side of the river so early in the day?"

The army surgeon nodded. "Some hurried errands, Mr. Kellogg. If time had permitted, I meant to come by your office for a game of chess. But Sergeant Ryan, here, seemed eager to get back to his drilling."

"Now Doc, you know it's Gen'l Custer and his paper collars that's worrying my mind," the sergeant protested. "If the general don't have a fresh collar for his dinner party, this sergeant'll be a private again before sundown." Ryan, who had been leaning against the rear of the ambulance, raised himself erect and looked respectfully at Kellogg. The sergeant was wearing an old gray flannel shirt open at the throat. His hat was a broad-brimmed sombrero which had once been white, but had been darkened to the color of dried mud by sun, wind and dust. Over his shirt he wore an Indian buckskin jacket. His powerful legs were encased in worn deerskin breeches. His only concession to the regulation Army uniform was a pair of well-greased cavalry boots into which were tucked the legs of his breeches.

"Glad to know you, Sergeant," Kellogg said.

"The name's Ryan, John Ryan." His accent carried a trace of Irish in it. "M Troop. The best in the 7th."

The ferryboat shook itself and began moving downstream, angling for the west bank of the river. In a few minutes the barracks of Fort Lincoln came into view.

"I suppose you're coming over to our fort in search of news for your paper," the surgeon remarked. He took out his pipe and began filling it with tobacco from a cloth sack.

"I'm hoping to see General Custer," Kellogg said.

"Ah, now that may not be so easy." DeWolf squinted at the sun, which had broken through the clouds. "With the weather clearing, he'll likely be down at the cavalry camp putting his boys through their paces."

Sergeant Ryan drew himself up importantly. "I happen to

know where the general can be found, Doc. If Mr. Kellogg would care to accompany me?"

"Certainly." Kellogg smiled. "I'd be grateful, Sergeant."

The ferry turned sharply, rolling with the river current, and slipped into the fort's landing. Wooden steps led up to a board platform where an infantryman stood guard. On the graveled bank, four Arickaree Indians wearing red woolen undershirts and blue army pants watched silently as Sergeant Ryan drove the ambulance ashore. "We might as well ride up," Surgeon DeWolf said, and motioned Kellogg into the rear of the vehicle.

A few minutes later they halted beside a long stable fragrant with the odor of hay. "Shall I get your horse for you, Doc?" Ryan called out.

"No, I'll be going by the hospital." DeWolf took a pair of leather bags from the ambulance. "Well, Mr. Kellogg, I may not see you again until we return from the expedition."

"We may meet again sooner than you expect," Kellogg replied mysteriously.

DeWolf hesitated a moment. "H'm. If you mean what I think you do, don't forget to bring along your chess set. They tell me there's always more waiting than action on these summer Indian chases."

"I'll remember that." Aware that Sergeant Ryan was moving about impatiently, Kellogg made a quick farewell salute.

Ryan said: "You'll be needing a horse, Mr. Kellogg. I'll see if I can confiscate one—hey, Sivertsen!"

A giant of a trooper, well over six feet tall with shoulders as broad as a door, swung around from a blacksmith forge. "Yep, Sergeant?"

"How many horses in there?"

"Half a dozen."

"Saddle one for Mr. Kellogg."

"Yeah, but Captain French wants these mounts down on the flats as soon as they're shod."

"Never mind about Captain French. I'm taking Mr. Kellogg to see the general. While I'm getting my horse, you saddle up. Then I got an errand for you in this ambulance." Ryan turned away, heading for the upper stables.

Sivertsen shrugged and turned to lift a saddle from the rack.

"Sorry to trouble you," Kellogg said politely.

"That Ryan," Sivertsen replied. "He thinks he runs the regiment."

"Somehow I got the same impression." They both laughed. "My name's Mark Kellogg."

"Jack Sivertsen. But call me Fritz. Everybody else does." He tightened the saddle girth and the horse was ready to ride.

While Kellogg waited for Ryan to return, a handsome young trooper rode up, leading three bay mounts. He began talking rapidly to Sivertsen, gesturing with his hands and glancing occasionally at Kellogg, who could not understand half the words the soldier was using. After a minute or so, the rider drove the led horses into a corral, and then went off at a gallop.

"I-talian, he is," Sivertsen explained in a drawl. "Captain Benteen's troop. Name's Giovanni Martini, but we call him John Martin. He sure can make pretty music on a trumpet."

Before Kellogg could comment, Ryan returned on a sorrel stallion which danced sideways when the sergeant gathered the reins. "Fritz!" he yelled to Sivertsen. "I want this ambulance driven up to the general's quarters right away, pronto. Packets in there for him and Mrs. Custer. Be sure she knows they're delivered."

"I got three more horses to shoe," the tall trooper complained. But he flung his leather apron across a bench and started for the ambulance.

"Ready when you are, Mr. Kellogg," Ryan said.

Kellogg strode to the horse Sivertsen had saddled for him, mounted, and swung around beside the sergeant, who was watching the ambulance sag on its springs. "Sivertsen," Ryan commented mildly, "is just too big for cavalry service. Hard on horses and makes too good a target. If we find any Indians this summer, they'll all be looking down their gun sights at old Fritz. This way, Mr. Kellogg."

Ryan let his horse go at an easy canter. They passed a long, low-roofed barracks with boarded windows. The sergeant explained that Custer had ordered all troops of the 7th out of barracks and into tents a week past, in preparation for the coming march. "As soon as we set up camp, it started raining. Always does."

"Well, the sun's out now," Kellogg replied cheerfully. "And warm."

They cut across the end of a deserted parade ground. Up slope, Kellogg could see the row of officers' quarters which overlooked the post and the river. Custer's would be the one in center, slightly larger, more ornate than the others.

Turning south, they soon left the fort behind. A grassy flat stretched before them to a field of white tents spaced in exact squares like a checkerboard. Beyond the tent village, platoons of mounted men were at drill—mounting, dismounting, wheeling, marching in circles, turning about, obliquing, charging. Off to the right, one troop was engaged in target practice, their carbines *pop-popping* faintly across the distance.

Most of the companies in the 7th rode matched horses—bay, sorrel, roan, gray. As the various platoons went through their evolutions they formed distinct masses of color against the greening grass—tans, browns, reds and grays—all accented by the sky-blue uniforms of their riders. Kellogg became so engrossed by the flow of color that he was almost unseated when his mount stumbled on a grass hummock.

"Easy, Mr. Kellogg," Ryan said, and pointed toward the

sun. "The general should be down by those cottonwoods."
He led off in a trot.

Suddenly they were in the midst of an Indian encampment, with dogs barking madly. There were no squaws, children or tepees—only scattered willow-brush shelters and an occasional drooping tent among the trees. In an open stretch of grass on higher ground was a cone-shaped Sibley tent with its fly folded back. Ryan dismounted, and Kellogg followed his example. They looped their reins over the limb of a small cottonwood. "He ought to be somewhere around here," the sergeant grumbled. They heard voices then from beyond the Sibley, and Ryan led the way toward it. As they topped the grass slope they saw Custer kneeling in the center of a group of Indians, scouts, officers, troopers and dogs —literally dozens of dogs.

On several occasions at formal reviews, Kellogg had seen Custer mounted. Now for the first time he was looking into the famous general's face, shaking his hand.

"You didn't waste any time, Mr. Kellogg," Custer said. The newspaperman stared back into a pair of keen blue eyes that seemed to be boring into him. The general's face was thinner than he had thought, sun-reddened and marked with freckles. A thick mustache concealed his mouth.

"There isn't much time, is there?" Kellogg replied quickly.

"No, of course there isn't. I've spent a busy morning here with the scouts, trying to get them ready for what we're going into." Custer removed his wide-brimmed, flatcrowned hat, pushed back his long curly golden hair, and mopped his brow with a red bandanna. He was wearing a fringed buckskin jacket, blue cavalry trousers and knee boots. "You might as well get acquainted. These boys are my eyes and ears, Mr. Kellogg. I wouldn't dare move a mile without them. Lonesome Charley Reynolds here, and Bloody Knife."

Charley Reynolds bowed gravely. He was a small man

with a down-curving mustache, and was dressed neatly in a white shirt, string tie and a black broadcloth coat hanging to his knees. To Kellogg, he looked more like a lawyer or a doctor than a frontier scout.

Bloody Knife was an Arickaree. His dark, heavy-lidded eyes were as penetrating as Custer's. His greased hair fell loosely over his shoulders like a black cloud. He wore a deerskin vest over a red undershirt. An upholstered long-barreled revolver was thrust inside his cartridge belt. His white teeth showed in the faintest of smiles.

"And over there is Lieutenant Charles Varnum, the military part of this scout outfit. You'll get to know the forty or so rascals as we go along, mostly Rees, some halfbreeds. Varnum keeps a loose rein on them, just enough to remind them they're drawing army pay." Lieutenant Varnum stepped forward and shook Kellogg's hand briskly. He was wearing a kepi at a jaunty angle.

Custer signaled his orderly to bring out camp chairs, and in a moment he and Kellogg were seated on the shady side of the Sibley tent. A dozen or so dogs roamed about, a large staghound dropping at Custer's feet. The general reached forward to fondle the animal's ear. "I suppose Clem Lounsberry explained the situation to you, Mr. Kellogg."

"Yes, sir."

"He recommended you highly."

"I'll do my best."

"Newspaper readers must not miss the story of this campaign. It may be the last big one. If the 7th can get at Sitting Bull and Crazy Horse, we can wind up the Indian wars for good. Put all the hostiles back on the reservations."

Kellogg started to ask Custer if he was certain that the 7th Regiment could do the job alone, but he held his tongue. Instead he said: "I don't understand why the Army doesn't want newspaper correspondents to go along."

"Politics!" Custer spat the word out, his mustache quivering. "I tell you, Mr. Kellogg, if I'm going to be scalped, I'd prefer it be done by an Indian rather than a Washington politician. But we shan't go into that now." He spread his legs, resting his hands on his knees. "Have you had any military service, Mr. Kellogg"

"I was a telegrapher in the Civil War. Field service in Virginia."

"Good, good. Then you'll be used to our rough ways on the march. I'll see that you're assigned a first-rate horse. You'll ride along with me, up where the action is." He was talking rapidly, nervously, as if trying to forget something that worried him. His shifting gaze caught sight of a trooper lounging on the grass a few yards away. "Ryan!" He shaded his eyes. "That you, Sergeant Ryan?"

"Yes, sir." Ryan leaped to his feet and strode forward to stand at attention and salute.

"What duty are you supposed to be performing down here at the Ree camp, Sergeant?"

"I brought Mr. Kellogg here, sir."

"Oh, I see," Custer smiled briefly at his guest. "Did you attend to those errands this morning?"

"Yes, sir."

"Mrs. Custer has everything in hand?"

"Yes, sir."

"Then you will report back to your troop, Sergeant. I'll see that Mr. Kellogg is well taken care of."

"Yes, sir." Ryan saluted and started to step back.

"Oh, Ryan. You better get into uniform. If General Terry sees you in that garb, he'll take you for an Indian and arrest you for jumping a reservation."

For the first time Ryan's face changed expression. His eyes fixed accusingly on Custer's battered hat and buckskin jacket, then he said softly: "Yes, sir."

Custer roared with sudden laughter. "Well, at least *I'm* wearing blue trousers, Sergeant. See that you do the same."

Ryan nodded solemnly and swung away toward his horse. "One of the best, Mr. Kellogg," the general remarked quietly. "The 7th would be nothing without sergeants like John Ryan."

2

Sergeant John Ryan

May 15

The reveille bugle awoke Sergeant Ryan. He listened to the call repeated, and guessed the bugler was John Martin, or Martini, the Italian lad with the big solemn eyes. No one else could put that special sort of sweet note into a trumpet call.

So it must be four o'clock in the morning, Monday, May 15—the day General Terry had chosen for the march out from Fort Lincoln. Ryan opened his eyes, aware that rain still dripped on the canvas tent a few inches above his head. Heavy showers had fallen Sunday afternoon, lingering off and on through the night. Hating the rain, he reached for his trousers and boots. Everything was damp—blankets, clothing, grass and tent.

He slid out of the tent, whipped a poncho over his shoulders, and surveyed the dismal dawn. All around him in the semidarkness, platoons were assembling for roll call. As he walked to his station, the rain-soaked sod squeaked under his boots.

His platoon was lining up, the men yawning, adjusting their ponchos, grumbling at the weather. "Attention!" His voice sounded hoarse to his own ears. He began calling off the names, listening briefly for a response after each call, remembering the men on guard duty or with the horse herd. He stepped forward, turned right and walked along the rank, eyeing each trooper carefully. "A bunch of half-drowned pack rats," he commented gruffly. "Not a mother's son of you wearing a dry thread. Barracks' coffee-coolers to the last man. If you aim to soldier with the 7th, you've got to learn to sleep dry in a river bed." He cast a baleful eye upon Trooper Sivertsen. "Private Sivertsen, at last inspection you were ordered to exchange your poncho for a larger one."

"Quartermaster issued me the biggest one in supply, Sergeant." In the gray light, Ryan could see Sivertsen's eyes blinking down at him.

"About face, Trooper," Ryan barked. He slapped the seat of Sivertsen's pants, which were soaked from raindrops streaking off the bottom of his poncho. "You back up to a fire, you'd steam it out," the sergeant commented. "Least you could do is button up the flap." He stepped back. "Fall out for saddles!"

A minute or two later the platoon, with saddles slung over shoulders, was marching unevenly over a soggy prairie out toward the horse herd. Rain blew now in a fine spray, and the sky was much lighter. When they reached the grazing grounds, Ryan dismissed the formation. Each man went to his own horse, took off the side lines and fastened them around the animal's neck, pulled the picket pin, coiled the lariat and mounted. In a few minutes the platoon was reassembled in a line facing Ryan, who had mounted his sorrel.

"Column of two's," he ordered, and they turned off toward a small stream flowing full to the banks after the rain. The men dismounted, unbitted their horses, and let them drink leisurely.

Across the flats, several hundred horses were now in motion, gruff commands echoing, men shouting to each other.

Smokes of cooking fires struggled to lift above the persistent drizzle of the rain.

"Prepare to mount!" Ryan shouted. "Mount!"

They rode back in a slow walk to their area, joining other returning platoons of Troop M, and drew up facing their mounted commander, Captain Tom French. Sergeants barked reports to the adjutant. Captain French saluted and conferred briefly with two lieutenants. The drizzle again turned to raindrops, beating against hats and ponchos.

A horseman approached at a canter, one elbow up to screen his face from the spray. Ryan recognized the horse—Comanche. Captain Myles Keogh's Comanche. At first glance, Comanche appeared to be only an ordinary buckskin—black tailed, black-maned, with a small white star on his forehead. But there was something in the way he held his head, Ryan thought. The horse had spirit. He was proud, a dandy like his spade-bearded rider, Captain Keogh of I Troop.

Ryan wondered what Keogh and French found to talk about, so slow and easy in the rain. After a few minutes, Keogh saluted briefly. Comanche spun nimbly around on the spongy turf and danced away as sure-footed as if he were on dry ground.

Captain French held up a gauntleted hand, his voice drawling, summoning his sergeants. They gathered around him, trying to hold their mounts steady as the animals shook their heads to clear moisture from ears and manes.

"The march out," French announced, "has been delayed for a day, maybe two."

"Is something wrong, sir?" Ryan inquired respectfully.

"General Terry's orders," the captain replied. "He thinks the prairies are too rain-soaked for wagons to travel."

Ryan made a scoffing sound in his throat, cut it off shortly.

"Did you say something, Sergeant?"

"No, sir, but I was just thinking, sir—the 7th never before let a little rain delay a march."

French smiled slightly. "The 7th isn't the only outfit going on this expedition." He added: "Cooks have been ordered to prepare regular breakfasts instead of coffee and hardtack. Return your horses to the grazing area, and after breakfast assign details to build fires for drying out wet gear. If the rain lifts, arms inspection and drill will be held as usual this afternoon."

Less than an hour later Ryan was seated with three other sergeants at a rough table under M Troop's cook tent. They were eating bacon, bread and molasses. Fog had replaced the rain, but a chill wind was blowing through the open tent, and they kept their ponchos on.

"What I can't figure," said Sergeant Miles O'Hara, "is why they won't let the 7th go on out and finish up this Indian war."

"Oh," said Ryan, "being as you are not a first sergeant, O'Hara, you're not supposed to know why."

O'Hara downed a swig of coffee from his tin cup. "And I suppose General Custer keeps counsel with the likes of you, Ryan?"

"General Terry, no less," Ryan replied. "He had all us first sergeants and the lieutenants up to headquarters tent yesterday and laid it on the line."

"I suppose he asked your personal advice?" O'Hara's tone was jeering.

"He showed us a map. This expedition we're going on, O'Hara, is just one part of the biggest military operation since the Civil War. See here, now. Lend me your knife." Using knives and spoons, Ryan laid out the operations plan as he recalled it. "General Crook is coming up from the south with one big outfit, General Gibbon is coming from the west with another big outfit, and General Terry and us are coming from the east. We'll all meet right about here." He put his finger where the knife ends joined. "That's the

Powder River country. We'll catch Sitting Bull and Crazy Horse right in the middle." Ryan slapped a fist into his open palm.

"That's the strategy, is it?" O'Hara declared skeptically. "You know what I think, Ryan? It'll never work. Too many cooks." He shook his head slowly.

"Tell you the truth, O'Hara, myself, I'd rather it'd be just the 7th." Ryan grinned. "With one general riding up front, waving his hat and hollering 'Come on, boys!' "

"Old Leather Britches." O'Hara nodded. "George Armstrong Custer!"

3

George Armstrong Custer

May 17

Before dawn on May 17, Custer awakened in the headquarters tent pitched at one end of the 7th Cavalry's camp south of Fort Lincoln. When reveille sounded, he was already dressed in his buckskins.

As the last notes died away he bent over and touched his wife's cheek gently. "Morning, Libby," he said.

"Is it a good day?"

"Foggy," he answered. "But it'll lift. We'll be striking tents in an hour."

"I'll be ready," she promised. He caught her hand, squeezed it, and stepped outside. The fog was so thick he could barely see the tents stretching away toward the river. The sounds of calling sergeants came clear on a raw, cold wind that made him shiver.

His orderly was waiting nearby with a saddled horse. The trooper saluted as Custer approached. "Good morning, Burkman."

"Morning sir," Private Burkman replied. "I saddled Vic, thinking as how she'd do better in the parade than Dandy."

"Good. Now I want you to bring Mrs. Custer's horse

around in about half an hour. She'll be riding with us as far as Heart River."

"Yes, sir."

Custer took the reins and swung easily into the saddle. He turned the mare toward the officers' mess tent. Lanterns flickered in the fog. The sky over Bismarck showed a faint gray.

He was wondering about General Terry. Terry had a good Civil War record, but that meant very little in Indian country. At least Terry had been honest enough to admit that he was no Indian fighter. And he had seemed sincere when he said that he was depending upon Custer and the 7th to do all the dirty work for him.

A strong aroma of coffee floated on the damp air, and Custer urged the mare forward to the mess tent. One of the cooks, recognizing him, filled a tin cup and brought it out.

He inhaled the steam, then sipped at the scalding liquid. "Best coffee I ever tasted," he said, and glanced up to see Major Reno approaching.

"How's the weather look to you, Marcus?"

"I've seen better mornings." The pouches below Reno's eyes were swollen. He was a thickset man, slightly overweight, his jowls trembling as he pulled his horse in beside Custer's. "Captain Benteen's patrol came in late last night from the west prairie. They say heavy wagons will mire down in places."

"Likely they will. Terry's marching the infantry directly behind the train. If the wagons do mire, the infantry will dig them out."

For the first time, Reno's stolid face lightened. "The boys on foot will have another score against the horse soldiers," he said.

"If the infantry don't like it, they should learn to ride." Custer drained the cup, and handed it to the major. "You'd better drink one of these. The day will look less gloomy."

Reno grimaced sourly and began to dismount.

Custer spent the next half hour riding through the camp, speaking to officers and men as he encountered them. When he returned to his tent, he found his wife waiting outside. She was wearing a riding habit and a short woolen jacket with the collar turned up.

"Are you cold, Libby?"

"More damp than cold. If the sun comes, I'll be all right."

He nodded toward the heights west of the fort. "The mist is already breaking up on the high prairie. Let's go to breakfast."

They ate at a folding table in the officers' mess tent, where they were joined by the general's brother Tom, Commander of C Troop. Lieutenant James Calhoun and his wife Margaret—Custer's sister—were also there.

"Is Maggie riding up front with Libby and me?" the general asked.

Mrs. Calhoun spoke for herself: "I'll be riding beside Jim, of course."

"If a drying sun comes out," Custer warned, "you may catch a lot of dust back there with L Troop."

"I won't mind. This is my last day to be with Jim."

Lieutenant Calhoun laughed. "You speak with such finality, Maggie. We'll all be back before summer's end."

"I know exactly how she feels," Elizabeth Custer said. "No matter how many times an army wife has watched her husband march away, she always wonders if this may be the last time."

"What a gloomy conversation," Tom Custer declared. He cocked his head to one side, listening to a rumbling which grew louder. "For a minute I thought that was more thunder."

"Quartermaster's wagons." Custer glanced at his watch. "Almost time for the buglers to blow the 'general.' "

Tom and Lieutenant Calhoun arose quickly. "Back to our troops," Tom said.

At exactly five o'clock the "general" sounded across the

mists. Commands echoed and re-echoed. Then, as if struck by a sweeping wind, every tent on the flats collapsed and fell to earth. In a matter of minutes, the men packed tents, poles, ropes and blankets into compressed rolls. The wagons fanned out for loading, drivers yelling at their struggling six-mule teams as metal tires cut into rain-soaked sod. Within half an hour everything was loaded and under canvas. The wagons formed in a widespread column of fours and began rolling slowly up the slope west of Fort Lincoln.

With plenty of free space now for maneuvering, the twelve troops and the mounted musicians of the regimental band formed in platoon fronts for a parade through the fort. Up from the Arickaree camp came the forty scouts, headed by Lieutenant Varnum, Charley Reynolds and Bloody Knife. Some of the Indians carried rattles and skin drums. Others played bone whistles. As they neared the spot where Custer was waiting with his wife and headquarters staff, the general motioned them to take the lead. He raised his right hand, the waiting buglers sounded the forward call, and the parade was in motion.

The nearer they came to the fort, the louder the Indian drummers beat upon their instruments. Some of them chanted war songs. Those with bone whistles blew bird-calls or eerie notes which sounded like wailing spirits.

Directly behind the Custers rode the sixteen-piece band mounted upon magnificent gray horses. At the instant Varnum's scouts marched through the fort's entrance arch, Bandmaster Vinatieri lifted his baton. A blast of brass and drums drowned out the Indian's weird and melancholy music. A wild burst of cheering swept along the column. The band was playing the regiment's favorite battle tune, "Garryowen."

Custer lifted his broad-brimmed hat, hurrahing along with his men. He sang some of the words, smiling at his wife, who smiled back at him.

Our hearts so stout have got us fame
For soon 'tis known from whence we came;
Where'er we go they dread the name,
Of Garryowen in glory.

The 7th Regiment came on the parade ground with guidons flying and horses prancing, every man sitting straight in his saddle. Along the parade route, families were gathered, waving and calling. Some of the wives were weeping; some were holding up their smaller children for a better view. A few of the older children had formed a little parade of their own, with handkerchiefs tied to sticks for flags, beating tin pans for drums.

After one circuit of the parade ground the Custers, with the regimental staff, swung out of formation to join General Terry, who was viewing the spectacle from a wooden platform.

"The 7th never looked better," Terry declared. "All the men seem to be in good spirits." Terry was black-haired and wore a short chin beard. He was a tall man with long, thin legs.

"Thank you, sir." Custer dismounted, assisted his wife down, and they stepped up beside Terry on the platform. Custer turned his attention to his regiment as it made its final turn around the parade ground.

Troop E, the gray horse troop, was passing by, its guidon flapping gaily in the breeze. Next came Troop I, led by Myles Keogh, his pointed beard neatly trimmed, his dark blues freshly pressed, his polished brass buttons glittering on his shirt. Comanche marched sedately, his hoofs keeping time with the beat of the drums.

As commander of the regiment's right wing, Major Reno rode a few paces forward of the next troop, with adjutant and trumpeter accompanying him. His face was without expression when he turned his thick neck to give the reviewing stand an "eyes right."

There was Captain Fred Benteen, his hair turning silver, riding with H Troop. And Lieutenant Edward Godfrey, a quiet, scholarly young man with tremendous dark mustaches, K Troop's commander.

Custer's sharp eyes missed nothing. He knew many of the men in the ranks by name. Sergeant Ryan of Captain French's M Troop, and that oversized trooper Sivertsen, and the dark lad who had fought with Garibaldi in Italy—the 7th's best trumpeter, John Martin.

The parade was coming to an end. The noise of drums died away as Lieutenant Varnum brought his scouts to a halt beyond the platform. Commands echoed along the formations. "To the left. March! Halt!" Officers and sergeants moved out to positions. Custer stepped forward, his voice rising as he shouted: "All married officers and men are granted permission to fall out for a short visit with their families in quarters. They will return to their troops immediately after the buglers sound 'assembly.'"

Troop commanders quickly repeated the orders. Scattered cheering followed, and the married men began moving away toward barracks and quarters.

Terry was nodding to himself, pleased by Custer's gesture. "The weather looks better," he commented. "I was just noticing the mistbows fading away and rolling upriver."

"The sun will be out," Custer replied confidently, "and we should reach Heart River by midafternoon."

"Frankly I dread the first day's march," Terry admitted in an undertone. "Been out of the saddle too long."

Custer suspected that his commander would have been much happier back in his comfortable department headquarters in St. Paul. He wondered why Terry remained in the Army. The man was wealthy, enjoyed fine living, and seemed more interested in art and literature than soldiering. Perhaps it was excitement, glory, the chase, the unexpected —the same things that Custer believed were what held him to the 7th.

He swung around and recognized the newspaperman Mark Kellogg standing beside the edge of the platform. Kellogg was carrying a black oilcloth bag. "I was wondering about you," Custer said, and offered a hand to help Kellogg up. "My wife, Libby. This is Clem Lounsberry's young man, Mr. Kellogg."

"Yes. General Custer has spoken of you," she said.

"Is Lounsberry here?" Custer asked.

"No, sir. He remained in Bismarck to get out this week's *Tribune.*" Kellogg smiled. "He gave me a farewell good-luck piece. His Civil War belt." He lifted the points of his vest. "Has a bloodstain on it. Clem says it saved his life, and he wants me to wear it on the expedition."

Custer laughed. "Pure superstition. But you should see all the good-luck charms Libby loads me down with." He frowned suddenly. "Do you have a horse assigned?"

Kellogg nodded. "I left him over by the stables. Our mutual friend Sergeant Ryan attended to the matter."

"Of course, of course. Ryan can arrange almost anything. Now you must meet General Terry."

Briskly and with no attempt at evasion, Custer introduced Kellogg as a personal friend who was accompanying the expedition, an unofficial observer who would write down what he saw. Terry was cordial. Nothing was said about newspapers, and if the commander suspected that Kellogg was a correspondent, he made no mention of it.

A few minutes later bugles were sounding "assembly." As soon as the 7th's troops were re-formed, Custer and his wife mounted and rode to the front. The regiment was now only one unit of the expedition. Terry would give the command to move out.

"Mount! Forward!"

Marching out of Fort Lincoln, the band played gloriously, "The Girl I Left Behind Me."

> Full many a name our banners bore
> Of former deeds of daring

> But they were of the days of yore
> In which we had no sharing.
>
> But now, our laurels freshly won
> With old ones shall entwined be
> Still worthy of our sires, each son,
> Sweet girl I left behind me.

On a high plateau west of the fort, the cavalry passed the assembled wagon train, artillery battery and infantry companies. Here a brief halt was made. After an inspection of the column, General Terry and his aides rode forward and joined Custer. Lieutenant Varnum, Charley Reynolds and the scouts moved out at a trot. In a few minutes the regiment was formed into right and left wings of two battalions each.

Custer and Terry led off with the advance battalion. The next two battalions angled to right and left flanks to screen the entire length of the column. Bouncing along behind the advance came the battery of six Gatling guns. Next rolled the wagons four abreast, with white canvas billowing under the sun now breaking through the mists. Alongside the wagons, the packers and herders drove pack mules, extra horses and the beef herd. Immediately behind the wagons marched the infantry companies, and then, falling in at the rear, was the last battalion of the 7th, serving as rear guard.

In this two-mile column, flowing like a ribbon across the greening prairie, were more than 1,000 soldiers and 200 civilian teamsters. Its 200 wagons were loaded with forage, rations and ammunition. There were 1,700 horses, mules and cattle.

Before the expedition had moved very far, the sun burned through the last of the fog. Up front, Custer glanced back to see how well the units were holding together. He motioned to his wife to look also. "A mirage, Libby." For a minute or more, about half the winding column was reflected into the vanishing mists overhead. It was as though men and horses were marching skyward. "Beautiful, isn't it?" he said.

"More awesome than beautiful," she replied, and added almost in a whisper, "they are like ghost riders in the sky." A troubled look crossed her face. "Could it be a warning?"

He laughed. "Only an omen of good weather for our first day's march," he assured her. " 'Custer's luck' still holds."

Soon the sun at their backs climbed high in the sky, glinting off the polished metal of arms and equipments, gilding the blue-and-yellow uniforms of the horsemen. As the land grew more hilly the column began to wind, avoiding rises and hollows. Ten-minute halts were called every hour. Occasionally troop commanders gave orders to their men to dismount and walk beside their horses. Some of the new recruits had trouble with unruly mounts. The animals were hard to manage after their easy life in the Fort Lincoln stables.

Several times the column was delayed when wagon wheels sank into soft earth, but infantrymen hurried forward with shovels and quickly dug them out. Two or three small streams had to be bridged with pine boards and poles brought along for that purpose.

The scouts reached Heart River about 1:30 in the afternoon, and a few minutes later Custer joined them. They were fourteen miles out of Fort Lincoln, an average distance for a first day's march over rolling plains. After horses and men toughened under the strain, they would be able to double that distance.

Custer selected a camp site on bottom land adjoining the river, a level meadow protected by high bluffs on three sides. Grass was thick and green, wood for campfires was plentiful, and clear water ran in Heart River. Shortly after the advance battalion moved in and dismounted, however, a cry of "Rattlesnakes!" spread an alarm through the camp.

Sergeants organized snake-hunting details, and by the time the wagons arrived, dozens of rattlers had been slain.

The larger specimens were mounted on tent poles to impress the latecomers.

Soon after the headquarters wagons rolled in, tents for Terry and Custer were pitched near the river. Orderlies quickly made down the beds, unfolded campstools, and erected portable stands for washbasins. Before permitting his wife to enter their tent, Custer made a personal inspection of the ground around the area to make certain no rattlesnakes had been overlooked.

While Elizabeth went inside to rest and freshen up after her hard ride, Custer walked around the camp to stretch his legs. By this time the entire column had wound its way into the meadow. Trumpets were sounding "halt" and "dismount." Unsaddled horses were rolling on the turf or were being driven out to graze by guard details. Woodcutters moved out with axes on their shoulders. Here and there white tents were rising. Mules released from wagons were braying and kicking. Smokes of cooking fires were already floating in the air. Spoons and coffeepots jangled. Weary troopers took brief rests on the grass, heads on their saddles, slouch hats pulled over their eyes.

To the unpracticed observer, it was a sea of disorder. Custer, however, knew his regiment, knew that within an hour the 7th would be ready for the most thorough inspection. Horses would be watered, rubbed down, picketed and under guard. Tents would be in proper alignment. Saddles and other riding gear would be neatly placed three yards in front of each tent. Woodpiles would appear in proper places. Sentinels would be posted on the bluffs. Trenches would be dug for mess fires. Beef cattle would be butchered, and meat ready for issue to each troop.

Confident of his officers and men, Custer returned to the headquarters tents. General Terry, Elizabeth Custer and Margaret Calhoun were seated out front, chatting leisurely. A light army wagon was drawn up nearby, shafts on the ground, its team already unhitched and driven out to graze.

A platoon of armed infantrymen guarded it. The sergeant in charge saluted as Custer came up.

"The best-kept secret of the expedition," Custer remarked to General Terry, "was that paymaster's wagon." He sat down in one of the empty chairs nearby.

Terry nodded. "If we'd paid off the men in Fort Lincoln, half of them would have swum the Missouri if necessary, to get into Bismarck to celebrate. We'd have spent a week rounding them up again for the expedition."

"Here comes the paymaster now," Custer said.

The paymaster, accompanied by several sergeants and a detail of troopers carrying pine boards, approached the wagon. In a few minutes they had set up a crude table, topped by an oilcloth. The sergeants laid the muster rolls of their respective troops upon it.

Custer strolled over and spoke to Sergeant Ryan. "Well, Sergeant, I suppose you'd about given up drawing your pay this summer."

"Yes, sir. I never thought we'd be paid off way out here on Heart River."

"Not much to spend money on in the places where we're going."

"No, sir. Sutler will get most of my four-months due, anyways. The same for most of my boys." He grinned. "That sutler better have a good guard going back to Fort Lincoln. I figger must be fifty thousand dollars in that wagon, and maybe half will go back. Be a nice haul for some highwayman."

"The guard will return with the paymaster. I'm sufficiently confident of their security to send my wife and sister back with them."

Ryan nodded respectfully. A bugle was blowing pay call. In a few minutes the first troopers would be lining up before the table.

That evening George and Elizabeth Custer dined informally in front of their tent. Except for General Terry and

Mark Kellogg, who were present as special guests, the dinner was a family affair. The party was made up of the Calhouns and Tom Custer; a third brother, Boston, who held no rank but was employed as forage master; and Autie Reed, a nineteen-year-old nephew of the Custers who earned his rations by working with the horse herd.

From where they sat they could watch the red sun going down behind the bluffs, throwing long shadows out across the encampment. The plain which they had crossed was bathed in crimson and gold, sunlit hills contrasting against darkening ravines. The dry air turned chill, enlivening everyone's spirits. After dinner was over, the group formed a semicircle before a campfire, and in a pleasant twilight the band assembled to play a short concert.

Custer's hunting dogs lay at their master's feet or frolicked around the tent. Soon after the music ended, most of the troop commanders came by to pay their respects—silver-haired Benteen smoking his pipe, Godfrey twirling his mustaches, Yates, Smith, Keogh, French, McIntosh and Weir. Reno appeared late, his face flushed, his manner aloof.

The meeting was no council of war; there would be time for that later, on the march. It seemed more like a summer outing than a military expedition until suddenly out of the gathering darkness came a cry of "Fire! Prairie fire!"

As the odor of grass smoke drifted across the camp, Charley Reynolds appeared at Custer's elbow. The two men exchanged a few words, almost whispers.

"Well, gentlemen," Custer said aloud. "Sitting Bull's forward scouts have fired the prairie. To let us know our first day's march has not gone unnoticed."

Benteen knocked his pipe against his boot heel to empty the ashes. "In three days' time," he drawled, "the old chief will know to a dot everything about us. How many men, horses and wagons are in this outfit."

"Let him know," Custer replied, waving a hand to indicate the strength of the camp. "It'll give him something to think hard about."

General Terry was gazing into the flames of the campfire which illuminated the faces of the group around it. "Perhaps we'll never find the hostile Indians," he suggested.

"Oh, the 7th will find them, General," Custer declared.

Off on the edges of the camp, details were moving out with wet gunny sacks and shovels to make certain the grass fires would not invade the area. Gradually the conversation changed to other subjects. Voices grew softer, varying from deep masculine to the musical tones of the two women. "Why is it called Heart River?" Mrs. Custer asked.

"I believe, ma'am," Lieutenant Godfrey replied politely, "it is so named for a hill shaped somewhat like a human heart."

"How interesting," she said, and was about to add something more when the shadows of two men crossed the campfire.

"Ah, Dr. Porter!" Custer cried. "I've been wondering if your medical duties would deprive us of your gay company."

"Snakebite and an ax wound," Porter explained. "I brought along my new colleague to get him better acquainted." Firelight fell upon the face of the other surgeon; an angular face, the eyes grave but friendly. His nose, Custer thought as Porter pronounced the doctor's name, is as badly sunburned as my own. "Surgeon James DeWolf."

4

Surgeon James DeWolf

When reveille sounded at three o'clock, Surgeon DeWolf pushed back the flap of his tent. The outer canvas was wet with dew. Stars glittered overhead.

While he dressed he could hear the camp coming to life, the rough commands of sergeants, a rattle of pots and pans, a jingle of harness chains.

Stretching and yawning, he stepped out into the cold gray morning of May 18. He took a comb from his vest pocket and ran it through his matted hair. Horses were coming up behind him. "Surgeon!" He turned at the sound of the voice, and recognized Charley Reynolds. On a pony just behind the chief scout was one of the Arickarees.

"Good morning, Reynolds."

Reynolds dismounted. "Major Reno said you were doctor for the scouts."

"Yes, for the right wing and the scouts."

"Foolish Bear here, he has a bad tooth." Reynolds smiled slightly. "I told him you could make it stop hurting."

DeWolf shrugged. "Let's have a look at it." The Indian

slid off his pony, his eyes fixed hard upon the surgeon. "Open your mouth," DeWolf said gently. "Which one is it?"

Reynolds translated, and Foolish Bear touched one of his incisors with a greasy finger.

After a moment, DeWolf said to Reynolds: "It'll have to come out."

Reynolds and the Indian spoke in Ree for a minute, and then it was agreed that DeWolf would pull the tooth. With no further preliminaries, the surgeon selected an instrument from his bag. He drew the tooth out with steady pressure, then held it up in the forceps for Foolish Bear to see. The Indian stared at it, disbelieving, until Reynolds took the tooth and handed it to him. "Keep it. It'll bring you luck," Reynolds said in Ree.

DeWolf saturated a wad of cotton with carbolic acid and gave it to Foolish Bear. "Tell him to keep that where the tooth was," he said to Reynolds.

The Indian then spoke to DeWolf, his hands moving gracefully back and forth.

Reynolds translated: "Foolish Bear says you have taken pity on him. He will remember it and take pity on you."

DeWolf was pleased. They shook hands, and Reynolds and Foolish Bear made gestures of farewell, mounted, and rode away quickly. The surgeon watched them until they joined the other Indians near the river. A minute later they were all splashing across Heart River, headed west to start their day's scouting.

After breakfast, DeWolf joined the officers in bidding farewell to Mrs. Calhoun and Mrs. Custer. General Custer accompanied them and the paymaster's escort for a quarter of a mile, and then came galloping back to lead his regiment across the river.

The wagon train was late in crossing. Poles had to be laid crosswise to form a corduroy roadway down each bank, and three hours passed before the ambulances and wagons were all across. The column traveled only eleven miles that day, to Sweetbriar Creek, the cavalry arriving hours ahead of the delayed wagons. Soon after DeWolf crawled into his tent, rain began pattering down. It was falling hard when he went to sleep.

Next morning, under the dripping mess tent, DeWolf found himself beside Mark Kellogg. The newspaperman seemed unusually cheerful.

"Did you bring along your chess set, Mr. Kellogg?"

"I did, and we must have a match when things settle down."

"Any time," DeWolf said.

"I'll come by your hospital tent one of these evenings. Up to now I've been so busy listening to Custer and Charley Reynolds swap tall tales that I haven't had a spare moment." Kellogg reached for a steaming sourdough biscuit and added: "Here comes the general now, energetic as ever."

Custer strode up to the sheet-iron cooking stove, sniffing at the sizzling frying pans. A poncho hung loosely over his shoulders. "Good morning, Mark. Surgeon DeWolf." His nose and cheeks were inflamed by sunburn from the previous day's march.

His fair skin burns as badly as mine, DeWolf thought. "General Custer," he said, "my doctor's eye tells me you have a painful burn. Have you tried glycerin and alum?"

"I've been using some of Bloody Knife's bear grease, but can't say it helps much." He took a tin plate offered him by a sergeant. "Do you prescribe glycerin and alum, Doctor?"

"It helps soothe the pain. I made up some for my own use, and I'll be happy to bring around a vial if the general wishes."

"I'll be grateful." He smoothed his mustaches back and took a bite of bacon. His blue eyes fixed suddenly upon DeWolf. "How would you like to ride up front with the advance today, Dr. DeWolf? Instead of plodding along in your ambulance?"

"It should be an interesting change, sir."

At five o'clock DeWolf was moving out on horseback with the advance. For an hour he, Custer and Kellogg rode along with Lieutenant Varnum and Reynolds' scouts. After the first ten-minute halt, the scouts divided and turned off on the flanks, while Custer's party waited for the forward cavalry battalion to come up.

They continued then across rough country, seeking a shallow ford across the Sweetbriar, but rains had turned the stream into a rushing torrent. Custer finally halted, shaking his head in disgust. With a rueful smile, he commented philosophically: "When you meet an enemy stronger than you, the only recourse is to outflank him. Gentlemen, we'll outflank the Sweetbriar."

After sending a messenger to recall Varnum and Reynolds, he turned the column back southward until the stream grew narrower and shallower. He led the way across, shaking his head again when his horse's hoofs bogged in marshy ground beyond. "Our wagon trains will sink to the hubs," he declared.

"The sky off there doesn't look too good, either," DeWolf said. He pointed westward. Gray clouds were boiling over the ragged horizon.

Custer lifted his hat, waving it as if to push the storm away. "We'll make for Buzzard's Roost and go into camp," he cried. "If I were superstitious, I'd say old Sitting Bull must be making some mighty powerful rain medicine."

They reached Buzzard's Roost within an hour, but the storm struck before the tent wagons could arrive. Sheets of water descended from the skies, followed by twenty minutes of peppering hailstones.

Except for wet trousers, the men came through the downpour in fair condition. The day was only half over, but they would have to wait for the wagon train. And as there was no wood at Buzzard's Roost for making fires, they resigned themselves to dining on hardtack and dried beef.

For DeWolf there was one cheering note in the dismal day. A Ree messenger arrived with a mailbag from Fort Lincoln, and in it was a letter from his wife.

His tent was full of mud, his bedding was damp, but he reclined there under a lantern reading his letter, and then took paper from his bag and began writing a reply:

> You must not worry for I am perfectly safe as we shall not see an Indian this summer, and if we do I shall keep safe and sound, and I carry a carbine and revolver so I will be armed in case of need, but I think it is nonsense to carry it, but I do so want to be sure and get back that I take every precaution to be on the safe side.

He was interrupted by the sound of boots squeaking on wet grass. A moment later the walrus-mustached face of Dr. Henry Porter appeared in the tent entrance. "DeWolf," he said gruffly. "You writing your last will and testament?"

"Letter to my wife. Come in. Sit on that box." DeWolf sighed. "Porter, what on earth can a man riding with Custer write to his wife without alarming her?"

Porter blinked his sandy eyelashes. He stooped to avoid the canvas overhead, and let his heavy frame rest on the empty ammunition box. "Can't say," he replied.

"I was just telling her I had a nice march today," DeWolf went on, with a bitter laugh. "And that I like General Custer and General Terry. I told her I am standing the expedition as well as General Terry—"

Porter chuckled. "Terry certainly isn't enjoying it, is he?" He rubbed his hands together to warm them. "Do you have a needle and thread, DeWolf? Ripped my blouse during that blasted hailstorm."

"Somewhere in the bottom of that bag." He pointed to

the medical case near Porter's feet. "This weather doesn't speak much for 'Custer's luck,' does it?"

Porter fumbled a sewing case out of the bag, his face ruddy under the lantern light as he stared back at his colleague. "You aren't the first one who's noticed 'Custer's luck' isn't starting out well," he replied softly. "Charley Reynolds told me the Rees are talking about it."

A rumble of wagons jarred from somewhere back of the tent. "It's almost dark," Porter added glumly. "And not all the train is in yet."

The next day's progress was even worse—only seven miles. Although they managed to find a camp site on high ground, the weather was raw with a biting west wind. And more rain fell during the night.

On the 21st, march was delayed an hour for religious services, the day being Sunday. By noon the sky cleared and wagons rolled easily over a drier trail. Orders went out to gather wood along the way. That evening when the column went into camp on a branch of Big Muddy, they built roaring fires for the first time in three days. Charley Reynolds and his scouts brought in seven antelopes, and DeWolf was agreeably surprised when his former dental patient, Foolish Bear, presented him with a choice steak for his share of the feast.

After supper, having no patients to attend, he strolled across camp to call upon Dr. Porter. He found his fellow surgeon working over a soldier's leg. "Unlucky chap," Porter explained. "Accidentally shot himself in the foot while mounting. Nasty wound."

The young man flinched when the doctor resumed probing for the bullet. "I say, DeWolf." Porter raised his head, his eyes blinking. "I wonder if you'd mind examining that trooper waiting there. The fellow's bunk mate was hospitalized with high fever before we left Fort Lincoln. The surgeon at Lincoln notified me by last mail that the patient broke out with a bad case of measles."

DeWolf whistled softly. "And of course this lad hasn't had measles."

Porter shook his head. "No. Most of the younger troopers haven't. An epidemic out here would just about finish the expedition. I take a look at him every day, and I've asked Lieutenant De Rudio to put him on isolated detail."

The soldier, who was standing patiently to one side of Porter's open tent, was wiry, all bone and muscle. His face was alert and intelligent. He came to attention automatically when DeWolf approached. "Sit on that camp stool, soldier," the surgeon said. "What's your name?"

"Private O'Neill, sir. Thomas O'Neill."

DeWolf drew a canvas chair closer and sat down facing O'Neill. He examined the young man's eyes and eyelids closely, then asked him to open his mouth. There were no signs of redness or spots on the mucous membranes.

"Are you in Captain Moylan's troop, O'Neill?"

"No, sir, I'm G Troop, Lieutenant McIntosh. But I've been assigned to take care of Lieutenant De Rudio's tent and equipments since I've been quarantined."

"I see. De Rudio's an Italian, isn't he?"

O'Neill smiled. "That he is, sir. When the lieutenant gets excited, he speaks more Italian than English."

"For an Irish regiment, the 7th seems to have more than its share of Italians. Felix Vinatieri, the bandmaster, and that young bugler—what's his name—"

"Trumpeter Martin, yes sir. He and the lieutenant go it sure enough when they tell about their service with Garibaldi in Italy. Captain Keogh can understand some of their talk. He served over there in the Papal Guard."

"So I've heard," DeWolf said. "Unbutton your shirt, O'Neill."

He found no sign of rash on the soldier's neck and chest

"If you can hold out another week, O'Neill, you'll be all right."

"Thank you, sir." The young man frowned slightly as he buttoned his shirt, then blurted out: "Surgeon DeWolf, sir, I'd like to ask you a personal question."

"Fire away, O'Neill."

"Some of the boys say, sir, that you were a ranker; that you studied to be a doctor while serving as an enlisted man. Some of us said it was impossible."

"No, O'Neill, it's true." DeWolf flushed in spite of himself, suddenly recalling the endless hours he'd spent toiling over thick medical books at army posts in Idaho and Washington. And then the two years of attending night lectures at Harvard after each long day's duty as hospital steward at Watertown Arsenal.

"I'm sorry, sir," O'Neill stammered. "It's just that I've always wanted to be a doctor myself, and didn't think I could ever do it."

"Is that so?" DeWolf wondered if he should advise the boy to try it the hard way. "Would you like to start as hospital steward?"

"If you think I could."

"A man doesn't know what he can do until he tries." His voice trailed off. "Seven years' hard work." He glanced at O'Neill again. The boy seemed eager. "When we return to Fort Lincoln, I'll speak to the senior surgeon for you."

"Thank you, sir, thank you." O'Neill's eyes flashed happily. He almost stumbled over himself as he hurried away.

DeWolf felt suddenly tired. He supposed it was the unexpected reminder of those seven lonely years which had brought him only to this hard field service. Porter, he noticed, had just finished wrapping his patient's foot with a bandage.

During the next three days the weather was fine and everyone was saying that "Custer's luck" had returned to the expedition. On the 24th, the column moved eighteen miles over a rough and rolling land covered with sage and cactus. Late in the day they crossed fields of wild primroses. When the horses' hoofs trampled the blossoms, a delightful perfume arose to mingle with the always present odor of saddle leather. Before the sun was down they made camp on Green River.

The river, Surgeon DeWolf observed, was aptly named. Along its banks were green willows, and westward as far as he could see was a high-rolling prairie carpeted with green grass.

As soon as his hospital tent was up, he attended two troopers suffering severe stomach pains. They admitted drinking alkaline water from holes during the march. He dosed them with pills and advised them to drink henceforth only from springs or clear, running streams.

With the change to good weather, the regimental band resumed evening concerts. DeWolf lit his pipe and sat down before his tent to enjoy the music. It was a beautiful evening, the sky streaked with varying shades of red and yellow. Along a sandy stretch of riverbank, several soldiers were splashing in the silvery water.

He heard footsteps, and glanced up to see Mark Kellogg rounding the corner of the hospital tent. DeWolf raised a hand in greeting. "Another patient?" he asked. "Or is this a personal call, I hope."

Kellogg laughed. He was carrying a small chessboard. "A fellow chess player, if you're in the mood, Doctor."

"By all means." DeWolf arose, entered the tent, and returned with folding chairs and table.

"General Custer," Kellogg declared, "insisted that I join him and his scouts for a late evening hunt for elk." He sighed, seated himself before the narrow table, and began placing the chess pieces. "After eighteen miles in the saddle, think of it!"

"So you declined in favor of chess?"

"I've been trying to think of a phrase to describe that incredible man. He never tires. In my notebook the other day I wrote that he was '*suffused* with energy.' "

"He is that. Poor old Terry, he tries hard to keep up with our golden-haired cavalier. But I notice that Terry limps about every evening and retires to his tent early."

Kellogg moved a chess piece cautiously. "Have you heard what the Rees have named Terry? Lame Hip."

"They have a nickname for everybody, don't they? Custer's adjutant, Lieutenant Cooke, told me somewhat proudly they call him The-Man-That-Always-Looks-Mad. With his fierce mustache and side whiskers falling over his chest, it suits him to a T."

A sudden shift of wind brought a merry strain of "Yankee Notions" loud and clear. Kellogg thumped his fingers against the table top in time with the drumbeat. "I had a talk with Terry yesterday," he said. "He wants to try to bring the hostiles back to the reservations before fighting them."

"He'd have his scalp lifted before he could get close enough to either Sitting Bull or Crazy Horse to hold a powwow."

"I tried to tell him that. I reminded him the hostiles were warned six months ago to return to the reservations. Instead of returning, the leaders have recruited hundreds more *from* the reservations." He watched DeWolf's chess move, studying the board carefully, and added: "They'll have to be taught by force, I'm convinced."

Next day under a cloudless sky, the column put another twenty miles behind it, first crossing rich grasslands, then ascending a long, sloping plain of cactus and prickly pear. A hot sun blistered DeWolf's nose and ears again, and he soaked them liberally with his mixture of glycerin and alum. On the 26th, two bridges had to be laid across deep-banked streams. This delayed march for five hours, so that they made only ten miles that day.

From his tent at sundown, DeWolf could see the badlands of the Little Missouri off to the west. Patches of red clay in the weird-shaped formations glistened like beacon fires in the dying sunlight. The area resembled some great, ancient city destroyed by a catastrophe.

Later in the evening he strolled around the camp, waiting for the evening band concert. Instead of band music, he heard the sounds of Indian drums and rattles and a wailing singsong chant from the Arickarees' area. He found Mark Kellogg standing nearby, observing the ceremonies with an amused smile.

"Good evening, Dr. DeWolf. It seems we have a variation in our musical entertainment this evening."

DeWolf was surprised to see Custer seated in the circle of Ree scouts, apparently enjoying himself amidst all the noise. The general's face, reddened by the sun, was almost the color of the Indians' skin, but his bright yellow hair was in sharp contrast to theirs.

"After the concert, or whatever they call it, there'll be speeches from each of the Rees," Kellogg continued. "Custer described it to me as a council. He suspects some of the scouts haven't been telling him everything they've seen."

DeWolf glanced sharply at his friend. "What does he think they may have seen?"

Kellogg shrugged. "I don't know, but here's Charley Reynolds. Perhaps he can tell us something."

Reynolds bowed cordially, a brief smile crossing his solemn face as he shook hands with DeWolf. "You've made a lifelong friend of Foolish Bear, Doctor. Don't be too surprised if he presents you with a charm he's making up for you."

"Fortunately for me, I pulled the right tooth."

Kellogg moved in closer, keeping his voice low as he

asked: "Charley, has there been much Indian sign recently?"

"Plenty," Reynolds replied curtly.

"General Custer told me confidentially that he felt the Rees weren't telling him everything."

"Could be the general got a little bit excited when he ran on to that hostile campfire yesterday, with no warning."

Kellogg nodded. "I was up there with him. The fire was still burning. He didn't like it." He touched Reynold's shoulder. "Talk straight to me, Charley. Do you think the Rees are getting spooked by too much Sioux sign?"

Reynolds snapped a twig off a willow bush and began chewing it. "Rees are good fighters, Mr. Kellogg. It's just that there're not many left. They hate the Sioux and will fight the Sioux—on even terms. But I'll talk straight to you —they believe the Sioux are thick as dewdrops on the grass, where we're headed."

The newspaperman leaned closer. "What do you think, Charley?"

Reynolds wrinkled his high forehead. His voice turned edgy: "I've stayed alive to now, Mr. Kellogg, believing in Indian talk." Again he bowed politely. "Excuse me, I have to do some translating for General Custer."

The music had stopped, and Bloody Knife was standing, arms folded, facing the blazing council fire. Custer had withdrawn, his face now half hidden by shadows.

As DeWolf watched and listened to the deep voice of Bloody Knife, the night deepened over Dakota. He felt oddly as if he were a part of a never-ending dream, lost in a column of ghosts moving ever westward. Firelight and shadows added to this feeling of fantasy.

And then he was brought back to reality by a man he could believe in, a restless man with keen gray eyes and a soft voice that seemed to be scolding both Custer and the Ree scouts—the voice of Lonesome Charley Reynolds.

5

Charley Reynolds

May 27–June 7

A light shower fell before daylight on the 27th, just enough
to settle the red dust along the trail into the badlands. Charley Reynolds was up at 3 A.M., sniffing the cool, rain-
washed air with pleasure.

He wondered what in the world was the matter with
Custer. The general had been acting strangely since the day
he returned from the East to rejoin the 7th Regiment. He
seemed to be suspicious of everyone, even the Rees. Perhaps
he had stayed too long in the East, living in crowded places.
Too many people spoiled a man for solitude.

In the old days Custer had been aloof, keeping his own
council. Now he was seeking council from others. He was
not like the old Custer. He seemed afraid to be alone, which
was a bad thing, Reynolds thought.

The scout took his saddle gear out to his horse, placed the
blanket, and began tightening the leathers. He would be
glad to see the badlands again. A man could imagine all
sorts of things while riding amidst those red cone-topped
buttes. Sometimes Indians would go in there alone to be
close to the Great Spirit, to pray for magic powers. The

badlands was a good place to go to be lonesome, and he guessed it suited him, because he was Lonesome Charley Reynolds.

The column camped two days in the badlands while pioneer parties went forward to bridge coulees and lay corduroy approaches on both sides of the Little Missouri. On the second day, Custer ordered Troops C, D, F and M out early for a scout upriver. Reynolds and twelve of the Rees rode in the advance.

By noon they were twenty miles to the south. They found some signs of recent Indian campfires and a few buffalo tracks. Reynolds considered the reconnaissance a waste of time, but kept his opinion to himself. These days Custer had to be always on the move; he was too restless to stay in camp while bridges were being constructed.

During the noon halt, the officers and some veteran sergeants gathered on a shaded grass sward. After rations of hardtack and pemmican, they smoked, talked, or dozed with their heads on their saddles. Custer sat with his back against the trunk of a cottonwood, staring glumly at the azure sky.

His brother Tom tried to jolly him with little practical jokes. Tom awoke the snoring Sergeant Ryan by tickling his nose with a straw. He lighted a wad of dried grass and held it near the boot sole of Captain French until the latter leaped to his feet with an indignant yell.

From beneath the lowered brim of his hat, Reynolds watched the prankish Tom. These were all old tricks of the Custer brothers. A year ago, the general himself would have been the ringleader. Now he only sat and watched his brother.

"Whoo-ee!" Tom finally burst out. "George, you're as solemn as old Charley Reynolds."

General Custer glanced at the scout, who was chuckling quietly. "Don't know but what that's a compliment, Tom," he said. He reached for his dusty hat. "Let's saddle up and move out of here."

Soon after they returned to camp that evening, another heavy rain began falling. Next morning the tents were still dripping with moisture. General Terry held up marching orders, hoping the canvas would dry out, but the sun refused to break through the gloomy, misty clouds.

The column did not move until eight o'clock, but long before that time Reynolds started his scouts splashing across the Little Missouri. As Custer rode that day with General Terry, Reynolds' only white companions were Lieutenant Varnum and Mark Kellogg.

After an hour of alternate trotting and walking, they reached the base of Sentinel Buttes. Ahead of them the trail led into a long gorge with rough, rocky ridges on either side. After studying the country, Reynolds and Varnum decided to divide forces, scale the heights, and flank both sides of the wagon route.

As they moved out, Reynolds invited Kellogg to ride with him. The scout had grown to like the newspaperman, even though he was always asking questions. After all, Reynolds admitted to himself, it was Kellogg's business to ask questions. Besides, the man had book learning and could talk about many interesting things.

All morning they climbed and descended, circling deep ravines, zigzagging up steep slopes. At noon they halted on a windswept rock, facing a higher uplift with patches of vegetation showing a wet green against the brown face of the cliff.

While they were eating cold beef and washing it down with canteen water, Reynolds pointed downward. Along the floor of the gorge, the covered wagons were winding like a jointed white snake, head and tail screened from view by boulders and trees.

Kellogg wiped his lips with his handkerchief, and drew a metal cigar case from an inside pocket. He offered a cigar to

Reynolds. The scout shook his head. "You never smoke, do you, Charley?"

"In my business," Reynolds replied softly, "to stay alive, a man must smell and see and listen like a fox. Awake or asleep. Smoking and hard drink dull a man's senses."

"I suppose you're right, Charley. General Custer told me how you carried dispatches from the Black Hills to Fort Laramie. Right through the hostile Indian country, all alone."

"I went alone because it's safer that way," Reynolds said. "That was a dry summer. No water anywhere. My tongue swoll up so I couldn't close my mouth. My horse about died."

"How'd you manage to stay clear of Indians?"

"Traveled nights. Hid in high grass by day. Sometimes war parties passed me so close I could hear 'em talking." As he spoke, Reynold's eyes were scanning the opposite heights.

"Do you have a family, Charley?"

"No. Had a girl once in New Mexico. I was always off somewhere scouting for the Army, so she wed another fellow."

"Where do your folks live?"

"No folks." His blue-gray eyes cut back to Kellogg, as if accusing the man of poying. But I'm a gentleman by birth." His lips smiled mysteriously under his down-curving mustache. He took his field glass from its case and studied the rocks above. "You ever taste delicious fat mountain sheep, Mr. Kellogg?"

"No."

"You may have the opportunity."

Kellogg could see nothing alive on the heights.

Reynolds added softly: "A pair feeding by that lower spot of green. Big horns on the ram. He's kind of a light tan color, like the rocks." He moved over to the Rees, spoke to them in their language, and then motioned Kellogg to mount up. "You and me, we'll go after the sheep. The Rees will keep us and the train both in view."

They were all afternoon tracking down the bighorn sheep. After passage became too rough for their horses, they dismounted. Reynolds warned in a whisper that the slightest noise might cause their quarry to panic, and for awhile they crept across the slippery rocks on hands and knees. When the scout decided the sheep might have scented them, he left Kellogg standing as a decoy, then slipped away silently. A few minutes later two shots sounded in rapid succession. Reynolds appeared, waving his hat for the newspaperman to climb up.

The sheep were so enormous that Reynolds and Kellogg had to butcher them where they fell, and then carried the meat down to their horses. They led the heavily loaded animals down one sharp precipice after another, until at last, to Kellogg's surprise, they walked right into the expedition's night camp.

They had a fine feast that evening, but it was cut short by another annoying rainstorm. To add to the discomfort, a cold northwest wind drove through the canvas tents. Before crawling under his blankets at bedtime, Charley Reynolds unrolled his buffalo coat and put it on.

Next morning, for the first time during the march, Reynolds did not awaken before the buglers. The sharp notes of reveille startled him from out of his heavy coverings. He knew immediately from the light inside his tent that snow must be falling. And it was the first day of June.

Snow showers in June were not unusual in this high country, but he had never seen so much snow so late in spring—two inches of wet whiteness, and the flakes still swirling thickly.

Bloody Knife and Foolish Bear had a smoky fire going under a camp kettle filled with remnants of the butchered sheep. Most of the Ree scouts were huddled under brush shelters, viewing the snowstorm with resignation.

"Big snow in Green Grass Moon very bad sign," Foolish Bear declared. "Custer's luck no more."

"Faugh!" Reynolds cried, and answered him in Ree: "When things go very good or very bad, you people say it's Custer's luck. Maybe it's Terry's luck, or Reynolds' luck, or Foolish Bear's luck."

Bloody Knife's shoulders shook with silent laughter. "Scold him good, lucky man," he said to Reynolds. "That one has been as full of croaks as a sick crow. He should go back to Fort Lincoln and live with the squaws."

Terry issued an order to delay march until noon. But at ten o'clock the great flakes were still falling furiously, adding another inch of ground cover. No wagons could move that day.

A biting northwest wind kept the livestock huddled in groups for warmth. The soldiers built big fires, and those on guard duty were relieved frequently. They stood around the blazing logs, stamping their boots in melting slush and mud.

When night fell, the storm seemed to slacken, but the morning of June 2, another squall was raging. Heavy wet flakes came down until midday, then suddenly stopped. Reynolds crawled out of his bed and walked up to Terry's headquarters tent. Terry and Custer were seated before a Sibley stove, blankets wrapped around their shoulders.

"Reynolds, is this all of it?" Terry asked grimly.

"I'd guess the sky's all snowed out, General."

"Then we'll move wagons across the creek this afternoon and have them ready for an early start tomorrow." During the evening the sky cleared, and Terry ordered reveille for 2 A.M.

At five o'clock in the morning the column was moving through dirty slush. A few hours later a bright sun transformed white-clad slopes back to green grass again.

Just before noon, one of the Rees riding off to Reynold's right signaled that he had sighted Indians ahead. Reynolds halted the scouts immediately and sent a messenger back to bring Custer forward. By the time Custer and the advance troop came up, three horsemen had appeared on the brow of a low hill a quarter of a mile to the west.

"One is a white man," Reynolds told Custer. "I'd guess the others to be Crows."

Custer looked through his field glass, frowning. "If they're friendlies, why don't they come on down?" He turned to the troop's guidon-bearer and ordered him to wave the swallow-tailed banner. A moment later one of the horsemen on the hill spun a handkerchief above his head, and the trio approached at a leisurely trot.

Reynolds urged his horse forward a few yards, keeping one hand on his booted rifle. "Who are you?" he shouted to the oncoming riders.

"Scouts from General Gibbon," the white man answered. He slowed his mount to a walk.

Reynolds jerked a thumb back toward Custer. "Report to General Custer," he said. He motioned the Crows to halt. They were both young braves. They wore their hair in braids instead of loose over their shoulders like the Rees.

"I'm Tom Easterwood, sir," the scout said to Custer, and pulled an oilcloth packet from inside his shirt. "Message from General Gibbon."

"Where did you leave Gibbon?"

"On Rosebud Creek."

"Between the Tongue and Little Big Horn," Custer said, nodding with satisfaction. "Have you met any hostiles?"

"Several small hunting parties," Easterwood drawled. "Twenty or thirty to a bunch. The big villages must be farther south."

"No fighting yet?"

"General Gibbon is avoiding a fight, I hear, until your column joins his."

"Good, good." Custer swung around in his saddle and waved to Reynolds. "Lead the scouts on out, Charley, but take it easy. We may be changing our course to join Gibbon. I'll ride back to discuss the matter with General Terry."

Half an hour later, Lieutenant Varnum overtook Reynolds with new orders. "General Terry wants us to guide the column to the mouth of Powder River. He aims to rendezvous there with General Gibbon."

Reynolds squinted at the sun, which was burning the last of the snow off the hills. "I reckon we'd better head for Beaver Creek and go south. No matter which way we go, it'll be rough on the wagons over that divide to the Powder."

Varnum lifted his hat and brushed perspiration off his forehead. "Terry says to move fast."

"All right, let's go," Reynolds said.

They made twenty-five miles before camping on a deep-green meadow along Beaver Creek. The stream was running clear with sweet snow water.

At five o'clock next morning, June 4, the weather was chilly, but before noon the sun was burning their backs. Terry took Custer's place with the advance, urging the most rapid march possible. He insisted that Varnum and Reynolds report back frequently on the condition of the route along the creek, and he sometimes rode forward with them to observe Indian signs reported by the scouts.

As the day progressed, Reynolds observed that Terry appeared to be unwell. His skin was pale, and he seemed to hold himself in his saddle with an effort of will. During a brief stop for nooning, the general stretched out in the shade of a willow, and lay there with his hat over his face, taking no food.

When buglers signaled time to mount, Terry arose reluctantly, took a staggering step, and almost fell. Reynolds sprang forward, catching his arm. "Just a dizzy spell," Terry said apologetically.

"I'll call Surgeon DeWolf."

DeWolf came up with his black bag, and with the author-

ity of his medical rank ordered the general to seat himself
against a tree. His examination was brief. "Dizziness. Rapid
pulse. No perspiration. You've suffered a slight sunstroke,
General."

Terry managed a smile. "What a climate! Frostbite one
day, sunstroke the next."

"For the sake of your health, sir, you'd best wait until my
ambulance comes up." DeWolf poured water from his canteen over a muslin towel and placed it on the general's forehead.

Terry looked embarrassed. "I'm not one to argue with a
doctor," he replied, and glanced up at Reynolds. The advance troop was mounted and ready to move.

"Go ahead, Mr. Reynolds," Terry said huskily. "You
need not report back to me for the remainder of the day."

Mark Kellogg rode out with Reynolds. "The old man
isn't feeling too well," the newspaperman said.

"He was trying too hard, I reckon." Reynolds let his
horse go into a trot. "Trying to outdo Custer. Can't be
done."

Early on the morning of the 5th, Sergeant Ryan reported
sighting an Indian on a nearby hill. "He was looking us
over," the sergeant informed Lieutenant Varnum. "He was
there one second and gone the next."

Both Varnum and Reynolds rode out on the gallop, the
Rees spreading out across the rolling country. They
searched along pine ridges and through numerous ravines,
but found only a few scattered horse tracks.

After the search was called off, Mark Kellogg rode forward with the scouts. In the afternoon he and Reynolds
went hunting again, bagging two antelopes and two black-
tailed deer. "No need for a man to starve in this country,"
Kellogg commented.

Reynolds nodded. "That's why the Sioux and Cheyenne
will fight to the death to keep it."

They slung the carcasses over their horses and joined the column in camp on Cabin Creek.

Next day they crossed twenty-two miles of sagebrush and cactus broken by enormous prairie-dog villages. As the column circled the pitted grounds, thousands of the startled animals stood on their hind legs, barking furiously at the intruders. Later in the day Reynolds sighted a small buffalo herd, and he and several of the Rees dashed in pursuit. They killed their first buffalo of the expedition, bringing most of the meat into camp on O'Fallon's Creek.

Custer met them at the Rees' campfire. "Good hunting, I see, Charley."

"We could have taken another, but no time to butcher. There's too much Indian sign out there today."

"Varnum reported the same. Tomorrow there'll be more."

"Yep. It's hostile country from now on."

"I'm ordering no firing of guns tomorrow." Custer's blue eyes narrowed. "We'd like to keep Sitting Bull guessing as to where we are. So no more hunting."

"I'll warn the Rees."

"Another thing, Charley. We're going to take the column to the Powder before dark tomorrow."

"Thirty miles?"

Custer's smile showed through his beard. "I promised General Terry we could do it."

"You may lose some wagons. It'll be the roughest country they ever did see."

"The drivers can carry them on their backs, if they must. Have your scouts ready to move at two thirty in the morning."

Reynolds and his scouts were in their saddles at 2:30. A chilly drizzle was falling, and an hour passed before the sky was light enough to show low-hanging clouds. Custer chose D Troop for the advance and pushed the men hard. He kept close upon the heels of the scouts, sometimes riding along with them. At times they could look back and see the remainder of the regiment strung out for miles, the files twisting and turning, zigzagging, climbing steep bluffs, descending into deep coulees.

Occasionally, because of looping horseshoe turns, the forward scouts could even hear the crack of whips and hoarse cries of wagon drivers in the far rear: *"Hi-ya, hi-ya, hup-hup, hi-ya!"*

Fortunately the threatening rain held off and the clouds proved to be an advantage, serving as protection from the hot June sun. Shortly after noon Reynolds halted his horse on the last high ridge. His gray eyes studied the panorama, reading the country as one might read a book.

To his left was a high ridge fringed with dark green pines. Below ran Powder River—a wide ribbon of yellow water flowing over beds of gravel and sand, lapping at boulders in its path. To the right, across a badland formation, were rows of dark forested ridges extending like enormous fingers into soft green grass-covered hills in the farthest distance. This was the country of the hostiles—how many, how warlike, only time could tell.

At 3:30 that afternoon, after thirty miles of hard riding, the scouts and D Troop watered their horses in the Powder. The men fell off their mounts from exhaustion, but their tireless commander had them on their feet in ten minutes, building cooking fires and laying out a camp site for the approaching column.

Not until 5 o'clock did Terry ride in at the head of the cavalry, and dusk would fall before the last of the wagons arrived.

From a comfortable position beside his campfire, Reynolds watched the tall, thin-legged general dismount. Reynolds was surprised that Terry had been able to make it all the way on horseback. He was also surprised to see him clap his hands together and shout vigorously to Custer: "Well sir, we've made it to the Powder."

"You had my word on it, General," Custer replied.

Terry peered at the sluggish yellow waters of the river, his eyes blinking slowly. "Now," he declared, "we can get down to the real work of this expedition."

Reynolds smoothed his drooping mustaches. You never can tell about a man, he thought, until things come to a showdown. Perhaps this general with legs like pipestems could handle Custer. Maybe there was more to this Terry than there seemed. The Rees, now—why, Custer just laughed when they tried to tell him what they'd learned from the two Crows who'd come with that scout Easterwood from Gibbon. The Crows said all the hostile tribes were gathered together and aimed to stay together in the Powder River country. They had sworn an oath to Sitting Bull they would never go back to the reservations. And there were so many of them, the Crows said, no army could defeat them. Custer had just laughed. Old woman's talk, he said.

No, sir, Reynolds told himself, Custer just won't listen to his friends any more. Maybe it was lucky for the boys of the 7th Cavalry that they had another general along. Maybe *he* would listen—that long-legged, sad-eyed Alfred H. Terry.

6

General Alfred H. Terry

June 8–20

On the morning of June 8, General Terry awoke at the sound of reveille. He felt remarkably fresh and alert, and was confident that he had shaken off the ill effects of his slight sunstroke. After his orderly brought a washbasin of steaming water, he seated himself before his small mirror and began trimming his beard.

He had just finished and was drying his face when the orderly announced: "General Custer."

"Come in." Terry buttoned his shirt collar and slipped into a sack coat.

"Good morning, sir." Custer's nose and ears glowed with sunburn, and he strode into the headquarters tent with his usual springy step. "As you may recall, General Terry, you told me last night just before retiring—"

"That I would sleep on our plans for today," Terry finished. "Well, sir, I've done just that—take that campstool, General Custer." Terry swung around and lifted a map and some papers off a folding table. "By my calculations, Captain Grant Marsh should have our supply boat, the *Far West,* tied up about where Powder River flows into the Yellowstone. I shall go down today with an escort, and if I find the *Far West,* I'll go aboard and steam up the Yellowstone to General Gibbon's camp."

Custer's face showed his disappointment. "I had supposed we'd join Gibbon and take the field."

"Not until we've scouted out the hostiles' concentration of forces. They could very well be up the Powder."

"Wouldn't a scouting party give them advance knowledge of our intentions?" Custer hunched his shoulders forward, his blue eyes flashing.

"No more than they probably know already," Terry replied coldly. "While I'm away you will prepare Reno's wing of your regiment for a reconnaissance up the Powder." He laid the map across Custer's knees. "About up to the fork with the Little Powder—here—then cut across west to Tongue River. If the hostiles are not in that country, we'll assume they must be farther west, toward the Big Horns."

"I'll have Reno's six troops stripped down to pack mules and be ready to move by the time you return."

"Reno will—" Terry cut himself off. His orderly was bringing in his breakfast. "You might as well dine with me," Terry said to Custer, and sent the orderly back for another mess tray.

"What were you going to say about Major Reno, General?"

Terry frowned. "That can wait." His face brightened again as he examined the food in front of him. "Our cooks seem to be celebrating this morning. Venison steaks, bacon, biscuits, peas, apple pudding and a slice of butter."

"The commissary," Custer replied, "is also confident of the arrival of the *Far West* with fresh rations. If Marsh has nosed his boat into a sand bar somewhere down river, we're in for some hard times."

"Captain Marsh," Terry replied, "can navigate a boat backward on a heavy dew."

Later that morning Terry left the Powder River camp,

with Moylan's Troop A and Keogh's Troop I marching as
escorts. Having no wagons to delay them, they covered the
twenty-five miles to the Yellowstone in rapid time. And as
Terry had assumed so confidently, the *Far West* was waiting
there—a 190-foot steamer with two powerful engines.
Aboard were supplies for the summer campaign—200 tons
of forage, rations, ammunition and medicine.

Captain Marsh came out on a crudely constructed landing to greet Terry.

"How long have you been here?" Terry asked.

"Since yesterday," the river-boat captain replied.

"Our timing could not have better." They shook hands.
"Do you have steam in your boilers?"

"The *Far West* can move in five minutes."

"I'd be pleased to have you take me up to the mouth of
the Rosebud, Captain Marsh. General Gibbon is camped
somewhere there on the north bank of the Yellowstone."

Terry thoroughly enjoyed the journey up the Yellowstone.
He liked the comfort of his cabin, the spacious bunk with
mattress, the leather chairs and solid writing desk. He also
delighted in the clean, well-cooked food and leisurely con-
versations with Captain Marsh. When the boat tied up after
sunset, he went to bed and relaxed into his first sound sleep
since leaving Fort Abraham Lincoln.

Next morning he received General John Gibbon aboard,
and they held an informal conversation on the shady side of
the forward deck. Gibbon reported on his march from Mon-
tana. The weather had been bad, the trails almost impass-
able. He had encountered numerous small war parties. His
troops had engaged in a few minor skirmishes, but managed
to avoid any hard fighting.

"My Crow scouts have convinced me," Gibbon declared,
"that the main body of the hostiles is gathering either on
Tongue River or the upper Rosebud."

Terry leaned back in his chair and watched yellow water
swirl past the boat's side. "I'm growing concerned about

General Crook," he said. "By our timetable he should have brought his column from Laramie into this country a week ago."

"Bad weather, perhaps," Gibbon suggested.

"It could not have been any worse than you or I met with," Terry replied quickly. "No, I think he may have had to fight. I'm sending six troops of the 7th Cavalry south along the Powder in a day or so, to scour the country for Indians and try to find Crook's column. The reconnaissance will sweep back north to the mouth of Tongue River. Perhaps by that time we shall have heard from Crook. Whether we do or not, we'll then strike out after Sitting Bull's stronghold, wherever it may be."

Gibbon nodded. "Perhaps another two weeks' delay will give this rain-soaked river country time to dry out."

"Gibbon, I'd like to ask your opinion, in confidence."

"Yes, General."

"Would you place Custer in command of this scouting mission?"

Gibbon's eyes enlarged in surprise. "I have a high opinion of General Custer's bravery and leadership. But he can be rash at times."

"And this of all times is no time to be reckless," Terry commented softly. "No. He won't like it, but I think I'd better hold Custer back this time. I'll assign Major Reno to command the reconnaissance."

Returning downstream in the afternoon, the *Far West* fairly skimmed along the Yellowstone. They reached the mouth of the Powder before sunset. At five o'clock the following morning, Terry and his escort troops were marching through a slow-falling rain. They rode back into the expedition's camp just in time to hear bugles blowing noon mess call.

Terry wasted no time in breaking the news to Custer that Major Reno would command the scout up the Powder. As the commander had expected, Custer protested vigorously. He paced up and down the beaten-grass floor of the headquarters tent, insisting that Terry change his orders and give him the command. "Reno," Custer declared emphatically, "has had too little experience in scouting Indians."

Terry let Custer work off his disappointment, then attempted to soothe his feelings. "I'll need you up on the Yellowstone to help plan the campaign. If Crook gets through, we can move then with a three-pronged attack, and you must be there for the final councils." Terry doubted if Custer believed him. Sometimes the yellow-haired general reminded him of a brilliant, strong-willed son with no respect for authority.

At three o'clock that afternoon Reno and his six troops of the right wing moved out with their pack mules. As soon as they departed, Terry ordered the remainder of the expedition to prepare to march to the Yellowstone the following day.

That evening Mark Kellogg visited Terry. "The horse I've been riding has given out," Kellogg told the general. "Your quartermaster says I must have your personal endorsement before he can assign me a replacement."

"We are very short of serviceable mounts, Mr. Kellogg," Terry replied. "You may have noticed some of the troopers are reduced to riding mules."

"Yes, sir."

"I suggest you select one of the more docile mules for your use. I'll write an order to that effect. It wouldn't do to have our only correspondent bringing up the rear on foot."

Kellogg stared hard at Terry, and was relieved to see a twinkle in the general's eyes. "I'll not deny it, sir."

"I suspected you were a newspaper writer from the first, Mr. Kellogg. And the fact that you were forever asking questions and scribbling in your notebook soon confirmed my suspicions."

"I've sent back only my daily diaries to Bismarck."

"By our official military couriers—but no matter. If I expected our mutual friend General Custer to do anything spectacular on this expedition, I might be forced to return you to Bismarck. More likely we'll all be back there in a couple of months without having been fired upon by a single hostile Indian. Go and find yourself a mule, Mr. Kellogg."

"Thank you, sir," Kellogg replied.

Next morning, June 11, being Sunday, the column moved late. After leaving the hills, the wagons rolled easily, and by nightfall they were all in camp at the junction of the Powder and the Yellowstone. Terry immediately went aboard the *Far West.* Henceforth, the boat would be official headquarters for the expedition.

During the following three days he directed the transformation of the expedition's camp into a supply base. Rations, forage and ammunition were unloaded from the *Far West.* Considerable amounts of these supplies were repacked for strapping on the backs of mules. He ordered the wagons to be partially dismantled and parked; they would be of no further use in the campaign. He dismounted the bandsmen and assigned their horses to troopers who would be going into the Indian country. The musicians and most of the infantrymen would remain behind to guard the base and perform messenger service.

By June 14, the left wing of the 7th Cavalry was stripped for action. Terry ordered a final inspection, and all nonessential articles, including sabers, were turned over to the quartermaster for storage. Next morning Custer moved out for the mouth of Tongue River with his six troops, the Gatling guns and a pack train.

As the regiment marched away, the dismounted band serenaded the troopers for the last time. The musicians had climbed upon a bluff so that the sound would carry a long distance. They played a medley of marching tunes, closing with "Garryowen." After the last pack mules disappeared around a bend in the river, Terry breathed a sigh of relief.

If all goes well, he thought, Custer and Reno should reach the Tongue River area about the same time. And Gibbon's forces were only a few miles farther up the Yellowstone. The campaign was beginning to take shape. He turned and went back aboard the *Far West*.

On the 17th, Custer's troopers made camp on the Yellowstone near the mouth of the Tongue. Shortly afterward the *Far West* pulled in to the bank and tied up. Terry came ashore and invited Custer and some of the junior officers aboard for a game of whist. For another day or so there would be nothing to do but wait—for Reno, and possibly for General Crook.

Not until the 19th did they hear from Reno. About sunset two Ree scouts came in with a message for Terry. Instead of coming down the Tongue, Reno had marched farther westward and was bivouacked on the Rosebud, across from Gibbon's camp.

Terry summoned Custer aboard the boat and told him where Reno was. "He's marched too far west," Terry said, "and of course has worn down his horses."

"I reminded you that Reno lacked experience in scouting." Custer slapped a gauntlet against his leg. "He may have frightened the hostiles clear back into the Big Horns."

"Nevertheless it's done. If he comes down here to the Tongue, his horses won't be in shape to move again for two or three days. So we'll have to change our plans. Instead of marching up the Tongue valley, we'll go up the Rosebud. I'll send the scouts back with an order to Major Reno to stay where he is and rest his horses until we join him."

"Agreed," Custer said.

"Have your regiment ready to move out early in the morning for Reno's bivouac. I'll go up on the boat. We'll soon know if the major found any Indians."

Major Reno had found no Indians on his long swing up the Powder and down the Rosebud. But as he was entering the valley of the Rosebud he had crossed the site of a recently abandoned Sioux village. "My scouts counted three hundred and sixty lodge fires. Charley Reynolds figured at least eight hundred warriors were there."

"At least," Custer commented curtly. "Were they well mounted?"

"There were signs of large pony herds, kept in corrals."

"In corrals?" Custer's blue eyes peered hard at Reno. "Then they must have been expecting attack. But from whom?"

Terry spoke up: "General Crook perhaps. Which may explain why we have not heard from him. Your scouts found no signs of Crook's column?"

"Absolutely nothing," Reno replied. "We followed the trail from the site of the village for a day and a half. Then Reynolds told me the Rees were becoming fearful. They believe all the hostiles are gathering somewhere southwest of here and that there are many more warriors than the eight hundred or so we were trailing. As it was time to start for this rendezvous anyhow, I ordered a turnabout."

After hearing Reno's report, Terry announced his intention to spend the afternoon questioning other members of the reconnaissance. He talked briefly with Tom Custer, James Calhoun and Charles Varnum. He ordered Charley Reynolds to bring in some of the Rees, and listened patiently while questions and answers were translated.

During the afternoon, as his cabin door opened and closed, Terry could hear Custer and other staff officers talking and joking in the outer saloon. The boat's barber had set up shop there, and 7th Cavalry officers were taking advantage of this last chance to have hair and beards trimmed.

After listening to the last of the Rees, Terry turned wearily to Reynolds. "What they've been trying to tell me, Mr. Reynolds, simmers down to this: 'There are many smokes along the Little Big Horn.'"

Reynolds face was somber as he replied: "Sitting Bull has many warriors. And all the signs say Little Big Horn."

"You're excused Mr. Reynolds. And thank you."

As the door swung open Terry caught a glimpse of Custer in the barber chair. A pair of shears flashed across his long yellow hair. A voice—probably his brother Tom's—drawled: "Remember what happened to Samson when he let his hair be cut."

Terry smiled to himself, then turned back to his maps and notes. He would wait for General Crook one more day. Then tomorrow he would bring Gibbon down the river for a final council of war. The plan was fairly well settled in his mind now. Sitting Bull's camp had to be somewhere in the valley of the Little Big Horn. The cavalry would go in first to seek its exact location, then hold until Gibbon could bring up his column in support. Confronted by such force, Sitting Bull should surrender without a fight.

The key to the success of his plan lay with one man, the leader of the cavalry. Reckless? Disobedient? Glory hunter? Well, at least no one questioned the bravery of that yellow-haired horse soldier, George Armstrong Custer.

7

George Armstrong Custer

June 21–22

Early on the afternoon of June 21, Custer, Terry and Gibbon sat down together in a small cabin aboard the *Far West*. Maps and papers lay scattered on a table before them. Here they would make final decisions for the campaign against Sitting Bull and his hostile Sioux.

"I regret," Terry said, "that we have yet heard no news from General Crook. We can wait no longer, and shall proceed with the forces we have."

Custer bent forward, studying the field map in front of him, tracing with one finger the valley of the Rosebud to where it curved westward toward the Little Big Horn. "I'm confident, sir, that General Gibbon and I can do the work between us." As he leaned back he ran a hand over his short-clipped hair, feeling unaccustomed bristles on the back of his head.

"We'll go over our plan once more," Terry continued. "General Custer will proceed up the Rosebud to the point where Major Reno discovered the heavy Indian trail. He will follow it until its definite direction is determined. If the trail turns toward the Little Big Horn, General Custer will swing westward. Meanwhile General Gibbon will move up the valley of the Big Horn to the mouth of the Little Big Horn. Is this quite clear?"

Both Custer and Gibbon replied affirmatively.

"Captain Marsh has assured me," Terry added, "that he can move the *Far West* up at least as far as the mouth of the Little Big Horn. There I plan to join your column, General Gibbon."

"I shall be honored," Gibbon declared.

Custer's blue eyes brightened. "This leaves me with full responsibility for operations of the 7th Cavalry?"

Terry nodded. "You may also have the battalion of 2nd Cavalry now under General Gibbon's command."

After considering for a moment, Custer replied: "No, I think not. The 7th can handle anything it meets. But I would like to have a few of Gibbon's Crow scouts. My Rees are not familiar with the Big Horn country."

"Six enough?" Gibbon asked.

"With the half-breed Sioux, Mitch Boyer, to lead them."

Gibbon frowned and spread his hands. "But Boyer is my best scout."

"I'll trade you my Gatling guns for Boyer and six Crows."

Terry's face revealed his surprise. "Are you certain you don't want *any* pieces of artillery, General Custer?"

"A battery of Gatlings would only slow my regiment, sir. I expect the hostiles to run away rather than attack us."

Terry tapped a pencil against the table's edge, his eyes blinking slowly. "Very well. The Gatlings go to Gibbon's column. If there are no further questions, gentlemen, this meeting is adjourned until tomorrow morning. In the meantime, both of you will receive written orders from me. General Custer, can you have the 7th ready to move by tomorrow noon?"

"Yes, sir."

"It has occurred to me that a formal review might put an edge to the men's morale."

"Agreed, sir. I'll so instruct my troop commanders."

Custer lost no time in returning to the 7th Regiment's headquarters tent where he found his adjutant, Lieutenant William Cooke, working at the field table. "Cookey," Custer cried, "Terry has cut us loose! The 7th is on its own. Leave off that scribbling and order the bugler to sound officers call."

"Yes, sir!" Cooke replied. As he arose, Custer gave him a resounding thwack on the back. "You didn't ruin your beard, Cookey."

"No, sir. I'm getting so bald, I thought I'd better leave some hair on my face for the Indians to take."

"Nonsense. I had my mane removed so they wouldn't think it worth while trying for."

In ten minutes the troop commanders were assembled in front of headquarters tent. "We move tomorrow at noon," Custer told them. "We'll march out after a formal review. Fifteen days' rations of hardtack, coffee and sugar, twelve days' rations of bacon and fifty rounds of ammunition for each man will be packed on the mules. In addition each man will carry on his person a hundred rounds of carbine and twenty-four rounds of pistol ammunition. On each horse twelve pounds of oats. Any questions?"

"Will twelve pounds of grain be enough?" Major Reno asked. "On my scout, I found the grass grazed down everywhere by Indian ponies."

"Then I recommend some extra oats be carried on the pack mules," Custer said.

"But, sir," Lieutenant Godfrey spoke up. "My company has been assigned to the pack train since leaving the Powder, and in my opinion many of the animals are so badly used up they'll break down under any extra loads."

Custer snapped back: "Perhaps your boys in K Troop haven't learned how to properly pack a mule." Noticing

Godfrey's face reddening, Custer added: "I did not mean to single out Lieutenant Godfrey for criticism. Few of the troopers assigned to the mules seem to know the art of packing. Well, gentlemen, you may carry what added supplies you please. You will be held responsible for your companies. The extra grain was only a suggestion, but this fact bear in mind—we will follow the trail for fifteen days unless we catch the Indians before then. That's all." He turned and was about to enter his tent, then swung around. "You'd better carry along an extra supply of salt. We may have to live on horse meat before we get back."

On the morning of June 22, skies were gloomy with a blustery north wind, but the troops of the 7th Cavalry were cheerful as they formed up for their last review. As soon as the men finished a hurried noon lunch of hardtack and bacon, the buglers sounded "boots and saddles." Custer started the parade with a ringing "Forward!" He rode to the upper end of the camp where Terry and Gibbon sat on their horses, and there he turned out of formation to join them.

Twelve buglers massed together behind the headquarters staff also wheeled out of the column. They played a fair rendition of "Garryowen" as the columns of four's pranced by with guidons fluttering. As each troop commander passed the reviewing generals, he saluted. Returning the salutes, Terry called out a cheering word: "Good luck, Captain Keogh!" "Good hunting, Captain Benteen!"

After the last troop and its train of pack mules passed, the buglers fell in at the rear. Custer offered his hand first to Terry and then to Gibbon.

"Now, Custer, wait for us," Gibbon cried, half in jest. "Don't be greedy."

Custer spurred his horse away, calling back with a wave of his gauntleted hand: "No, I will not."

For four hours the column moved southward up the valley of the Rosebud, fittingly named for masses of wild rosebushes which flourished among cottonwoods and willows bordering the narrow creek.

In late afternoon Custer signaled a halt at the base of a steep bluff where the scouts had reported plenty of wood, water and grass. He dismounted and strode rapidly around the camp. As tents had been left at the Yellowstone base, the men were already at work making beds of willow limbs and grass.

Along the creek, Custer encountered Surgeon DeWolf, who was carefully trimming a rose with a pair of surgical scissors. "Collecting botanical specimens, Dr. DeWolf?"

"I thought I might press one of these sweet-scented roses and enclose it in a letter to my wife," DeWolf replied. "Perhaps it might reassure her."

"An excellent idea." Custer leaned down to sniff the blossom. "Would you prepare one for me, to send to my wife?"

"Of course."

Custer resumed his rapid walk, calling back over his shoulder: "We'll be sending messages and letters back in a couple of days."

When he returned to the site which he had selected for headquarters, he found that his orderly had prepared a lean-to of poles and branches. Adjutant Cooke was seated on a nearby boulder, already at work over the day's reports. "Officers' meeting right after supper, Cookey," he announced, with a note of weariness in his voice. "Notify them by messenger." He removed his gauntlets and slapped them nervously against his leg. "I think I'll lie down for awhile."

Lieutenant Cooke turned around in surprise. "Are you ill, sir?"

"No. Just tired."

The sun was setting in a bank of stormy red-streaked clouds when the troop commanders assembled at a campfire in front of Custer's bivouac. "Stand or sit, as you please, gentlemen," the general said. He sat on his blanket with his legs jackknifed in front of him. His face looked gray in the fading daylight. He spoke slowly, with none of his usual curtness. "You may have noticed that you were summoned here by messenger. Until further notice, no bugle calls will be sounded except in emergencies. As we are looking for the hostiles, so are they watching for us. Let us do all we can to keep our approach a surprise."

He let his chin rest on his knees, pausing as if he were gathering his energies. "Now, I understand there's been some criticism because I have declined to accept General Terry's offer of the 2nd Cavalry. That was done because I'm sure the 7th can whip any force of Indians. If we can't, no other regiment can. The addition of any cavalry would only create friction, slow us down. I also understand there's been criticism because I cut loose the Gatling guns. That was done for the same reason—to assure us of rapid mobility."

His eyes swept around the circle in front of him. "As of now, the right and left wings are abolished. Each troop commander will report directly to me. Each commander will be responsible for his troop. I shall rely upon your individual judgments, discretions and loyalties. I ask each one of you to make any suggestions to me that you see fit."

There was a dead silence. I suppose, Custer thought, this is the first time I've ever asked my officers to make suggestions to me. "Well, gentlemen," he added then, his voice carrying some of its old brusqueness, "I have one criticism to make of you. This regiment traveled only twelve miles today. We should have done much better. I lay the blame on the pack trains. From now on, I want to see better packing." Across the dancing firelight he saw the alert young face of Lieutenant Godfrey, half concealed by a pair of wildly curling mustaches. "I suggest," Custer concluded mockingly, "that if any of you wish to learn how to pack a mule properly, you consult our junior lieutenant, Edward Godfrey."

8

Lieutenant
Edward Godfrey

June 22–25

Lieutenant Godfrey was in a dark mood when he left Custer's campfire. He walked slowly, picking his way in the shadows toward K Troop's camping area. Hearing footsteps behind him, he paused, glanced back, and in reflected firelight recognized his friend Lieutenant George Wallace.

"Godfrey, is that you?"

"Yes, George."

Wallace stumbled over a sagebrush, then came alongside. "What did you think of that meeting, Godfrey?"

"I can't believe it was Custer. He acted as if he wanted our help."

"Godfrey, I believe General Custer is going to be killed."

"Why? What makes you think that?"

"Because," Wallace replied soberly, "I've never heard him talk the way he did tonight. Explaining his actions, asking our advice."

Godfrey refused to admit that he, too, was worried. "Oh, perhaps he has a fever or something. He'll be the same old Custer tomorrow."

Next morning, to Godfrey's relief, Custer did seem to be

his old self again. He started the march at five o'clock with a jaunty gesture, riding out with two color-bearers. One carried the regimental flag, an eagle on a field of blue bordered with yellow. The other bore Custer's personal headquarters guidon, a red-and-blue swallowtail with crossed sabers. Custer's luck, Godfrey said to himself. His Civil War guidon.

Feeling somewhat reassured about his commander, Godfrey ordered his men to mount. They formed four's, and in a few minutes fell in the line of march.

About seven o'clock that morning the column halted and orders came down the line for troop commanders to ride forward. As he neared the advance position Godfrey observed that all around were signs of a recently abandoned Indian village, the one Reno had reported finding on his scout. Yellowed circles on the grass revealed where tepees had stood, and there were numerous remains of charred fires, piles of buffalo bones.

"We start trailing here," Custer announced to the officers gathered around him on their horses. "From now on we must move fast. Look to your pack mules when you return to your troops, and see that there are no delays."

He waved to Charley Reynolds to move out with the Rees, then put the column back in motion.

Godfrey trotted his horse back to his troop and then pulled aside until the pack mules came up. He looked the packs over carefully, glancing in surprise at one of the troopers walking alongside. "Private O'Neill," he said. "Are you returned to regular duty?"

"Yes, sir. Since we stowed the tents." The wiry trooper slapped a mule back into line with a switch. "Surgeon De-Wolf gave me a clean bill of health."

"No measles, eh?"

"No, sir. If the lieutenant has a moment, sir, I'd like to request permission to put in for hospital steward at first chance."

Godfrey checked his reins, dancing his horse sideways.

"You think you'd like doctoring better than mule driving O'Neill?"

"Yes, sir." He smiled. "Surgeon DeWolf has promised to speak for me."

Godfrey nodded. "Very well, O'Neill. See me when we get back to Fort Lincoln."

After thirty-three miles of marching, they halted that evening in a wooded valley. For hundreds of yards around, the grass had been cropped close by Indian ponies. Later when Godfrey saw Charley Reynolds, he asked the scout how many mounts he thought the Indians had.

"More than a thousand," Reynolds replied. "And the Crows tell me we'll find an even bigger abandoned camp about ten miles south."

Next morning, the 24th, Godfrey's K Troop marched near the advance, just behind Captain French's M Troop. In about two hours they reached the large abandoned camp reported by the scouts and a halt was ordered while the Crows and Rees fanned out to search the area.

Godfrey dismounted his men and then rode up to a circular pole frame which surrounded a large upright pine trunk in the center. Reynolds was there with Custer and Captain French. "Sun Dance lodge," Reynolds said. "Not over a week ago. They had a big time here. This bunch will be raring to fight."

"How many?" Custer asked.

Reynolds compressed his lips, staring up and down the grassed valley at the worn tepee circles. "At least another thousand."

"The 7th can handle the warriors from both camps," Custer declared, "even if they're together, which they may not be."

"Captain French!" The call came from a group of enlisted men who had been poking about in heaps of dried sage and sweet grass on the floor of the abandoned Sun Dance lodge.

Sergeant John Ryan strode forward, displaying a scalp on the end of a stick. "Looks like a white man's," Ryan said.

"What do you think, Reynolds?" French asked.

Reynolds examined the scalp carefully. "Soldier's, I'd guess. Taken not more'n a week or two weeks ago."

"Could have been one of Gibbon's stragglers," Godfrey suggested.

"More likely one of Crook's men," Custer said. "Terry was probably right. Crook could have run into a bunch over in the Big Horn country."

"Then there may be more," Godfrey said, and joined the soldiers who were still stirring about in the debris. "Private Sivertsen, do you see any signs of other scalps?"

The big trooper stood at attention, towering over Godfrey. "No, sir. I thought this was one, but it's just a piece of animal skin with some kind of pictures on it." He handed a curled scrap of soft leather to the lieutenant.

Godfrey studied the red-and-blue markings on the piece of deerskin. He could see a horse with its legs thrust out front and back like a toy rocking horse. In front of the animal was a figure on foot, a soldier with blue trousers. On back of the horse was a naked rider, with a line drawn to the soldier's chest—like an arrow. Floating in the air behind the outline of the rider was a strange, dark object with horns.

"Reynolds, what on earth do you make of this?"

The scout peered at the pictograph for a moment, then turned toward Custer, his voice betraying his excitement. "That's a bull buffalo behind the rider," he declared. "A sitting bull!"

Custer moved in closer. "Sitting Bull. I've heard the old devil likes to draw pictures of his killings."

"He's counting *coup* on a soldier," Reynolds said.

Godfrey stared about him in wonderment. "Then this was Sitting Bull's Sun Dance lodge!" He saw Mark Kellogg approaching.

"May I have a look at that pictograph?" Kellogg asked.

A horseman came in at a gallop, Adjutant Cooke. "General Custer," Cooke called as he reined up sharply. "The Crows who went out at daylight have just returned. They think they've sighted a hostile camp."

"Good!" Custer's eyes brightened. "Captain French, have that scalp buried properly." He turned to his orderly. "Burkman, stick my headquarters flag in the ground there, and tell the troop commanders to gather on it." He rubbed his hands together. "Gentlemen, the 7th is about ready for some action."

The officers' conference was brief. Lieutenant Varnum came in with the half-breed Mitch Boyer and the Crow scouts. They reported sighting smokes in a valley, probably thirty miles to the west. "That would be the Little Big Horn," Custer said. He was standing a few feet from his guidon, which was whipping in a stiff south breeze. "For the remainder of the day, it will be a forced march," he continued quietly. "We'll try to make it to the divide. Dismissed."

As the assembly broke up, a sudden wind gust toppled the guidon across Godfrey's path. He bent down, picked it up, and thrust the staff back into its hole in the dry ground. Again the wind swept it down. This time Godfrey spun the staff into a fresh hole, supporting the guidon against a sagebrush.

He glanced up and saw Lieutenant Wallace staring at him. "That's an ill omen, Godfrey," the lieutenant said, his voice almost a whisper.

"What—oh, you mean the flag blowing down."

"A flag falling toward the rear is a sign of a defeat," Wallace declared.

Godfrey forced a laugh. "You're getting to be as spooked as the Rees, George. It was just the wind." But he recalled that old superstition from somewhere, and felt suddenly uneasy.

They resumed march under a hot sun, with hourly stops cut from the usual ten minutes to five minutes. A blind man could have followed the Indian trail now. In some places it was a hundred yards wide, pockmarked with hoof prints and scratched by many travois poles. At midday Custer passed back an order for troops to spread out and walk their horses on grassy stretches, to keep down revealing clouds of dust.

They marched until sundown, halting under cover of a bluff. Coffee fires were kept small and were extinguished as soon as darkness fell.

About nine o'clock, after guards were posted and reports made, some of the officers gathered in a grove of box elders. They sat with their backs against the tree trunks, resting and talking.

"We didn't make it to the divide, did we?" Godfrey asked.

"No," replied Captain Benteen. "Charley Reynolds told me it was another ten miles. My guess is we'll see it though, before daylight."

"How so?" asked Captain Keogh.

"Night march," Benteen replied. He scratched a wooden match on his trousers and lit his pipe, the flame revealing his sun-browned face framed by a mass of white hair.

"Have you heard anything?" Godfrey asked.

"No, but it figures up. Custer will want to be there by daylight so he can look down at that hostile camp."

"Comanche won't like it," Keogh said. "He's not a night horse."

"How's the old claybank holding up?" Benteen asked.

"He could outrun any piece of Indian horseflesh in this country. Mustangs included."

"He may have a chance to prove that tomorrow or next day. Hey, who's that?"

Somebody had stumbled across a ditch. "Mark Kellogg," a voice answered out of the darkness. "I'm looking for headquarters," the newspaperman explained. "I heard General Custer was sending messengers back to the Yellowstone tonight."

"Over to your right, hundred yards or so," Godfrey told him.

"Say, Kellogg," Benteen remarked, "I hear you been sending pieces back to the Bismarck paper about us. What's the latest news?"

Kellogg laughed. "Not much. I scribbled out a little filler material this morning when we left the Rosebud. Told my editor that by the time it reaches him we will have met the red devils, and that I'll be in at the death."

"Good heavens, man," Keogh protested, "you didn't really say you'd be in at the death?"

"You have to be dramatic when you write for a newspaper," Kellogg explained, and turned off in the darkness in the general direction of Custer's headquarters bivouac.

"He's not a bad sort," Keogh said. "For a civilian."

Benteen knocked his pipe out, yawned, and removed his boots. "See here, fellows. If you aim to be collecting any sleep, you better be doing it soon—"

A voice drawled out of the night: "They're over there by those trees."

"Captain Benteen, Captain Keogh, Lieutenant Godfrey!"

"Over here!"

"The general's compliments," cried the familiar voice of Custer's orderly, "and he wants to see all officers at headquarters immediately."

It was as Captain Benteen had foreseen. Custer ordered a night march. For a few minutes all was confusion. With saddles and bridles in their hands, sleepy men stumbled through the darkness, hurrying to their horses. As soon as mounts were girthed and bitted, the column moved out.

The night was warm, with no wind; the trail powdery with dust that at times suffocated the rear riders. No wonder, Godfrey thought, Custer had decided to travel by darkness. In daylight, the dust cloud they were making would have revealed the column's movement for miles.

Godfrey tied a handkerchief over his nose, straining his eyes to follow the faint, moving silhouettes of the troop ahead of his. At times he could see nothing but blackness. Only the banging of a loose frying pan on one of the horses just ahead enabled him to keep to the trail.

After three hours of steady plodding, the command halted. Godfrey dismounted his men and ordered them to rest as best they could beside their mounts. When dawn came, he could see a ridge directly in front. At its base flowed a small stream. A messenger brought an order permitting a few small fires for coffee, provided they were extinguished as soon as the water warmed.

Off to the right, Benteen already had a blaze going, and Godfrey strolled over to borrow a cup of coffee.

"It tastes like suds from a washpot," Benteen grumbled. "Water's alkaline."

Godfrey took a sip, rolling it in his mouth, then swallowed doubtfully. He saw Custer's orderly approaching. "What now?" Benteen growled.

"The general wants your bugler assigned to him," the orderly reported.

"He *would* take the best trumpeter in the outfit. Hey, where's Garibaldi? Trumpeter John Martin!"

9

Trumpeter John Martin

June 25, 8 A.M.–12 noon

John Martin guided his horse through the dismounted troop toward Custer's headquarters' flag. It was like in the old country, he thought, when Garibaldi had chosen him to be his drummer boy at Monte Saello. Then he was fifteen years old and his name was Giovanni Martini. Now he was more than twenty, he was an American, his name was John Martin, and General Custer had chosen him to be his orderly trumpeter.

He held himself proudly erect as he rode up to the place where Custer was talking to Charley Reynolds and some of the Ree scouts. He dismounted, picketed his horse, and walked toward the general. Custer was dressed in a blue-gray flannel shirt, buckskin trousers, high knee boots and a broad-brimmed hat.

Except for Custer's uniform, it was remarkable how much he looked like Garibaldi. Lieutenant De Rudio had often spoken of the resemblance—the same shape of beard, curly hair, eyes that flashed fire under excitement or anger.

"Sir, Trumpeter Martin reporting for duty."

Custer, who was kneeling in a circle with the scouts,

glanced up at Martin. He waved one hand slightly and indicated that the bugler should remain at ease and await further orders.

Martin sat down on a grass hummock, keeping his eyes on the general.

Bloody Knife was speaking rapidly in Ree, and making signs with his hands.

"What's that he says?" Custer demanded.

Reynolds translated: "He says we'll find enough Sioux along the Little Big Horn to keep us fighting two or three days."

Custer smiled. "I guess we'll get through with them in one day." He stood up, stretching himself. "All right, Charley, you can move out. But keep under cover. We don't want them to see us today." He turned to Martin. "You'll not need your trumpet until we know the hostiles have seen us. Mount up, and ride with me."

To Martin's surprise, Custer leaped on an unsaddled horse and started on a ride through the camp. As the general came to each troop commander he stopped for a moment, spoke softly, and announced that the column would march out in a few minutes.

At 8:30 the column was on the trail again, moving in a slow walk so as not to stir up too much dust. At Custer's order, Martin rode directly behind the general and Adjutant Cooke.

Two hours later they turned off the trail into a ravine and Custer signaled a halt. "We'll be well hidden here," he said to Lieutenant Cooke. "Order officers to dismount their men, but keep saddles on. Post guards on the ridge, but impress upon them they are to keep in concealment. No straggling whatever to be permitted."

Cooke shouted a command back to the forward troop to dismount. "Pass it on!"

The bearded adjutant scribbled Custer's orders on the leaf of a notebook, ripped it out, and handed it to Martin. "Take this back to the first troop commander. After he reads it, take it on to the next, and so on to the rear of the column."

Saluting briskly, Martin turned his horse and started back along the column. Along the way he had to keep turning his horse into the sagebrush to avoid trampling dismounted soldiers so weary for sleep they had flung themselves on the ground with their bridle reins over their arms and their hats over their eyes.

When Martin returned to the advance position, he saw that Lieutenant Varnum had just come in with the Crows to report to Custer. Varnum's uniform was covered with dust, and he kept dabbing at moisture in his red-rimmed eyes. "No, sir, I could not see them," Varnum was saying. "But the Crows swear they could see an immense pony herd in the valley of the Little Big Horn. They told me to 'look for worms.' I tried, but my eyes are pretty sore."

"How long have you gone without sleep, Varnum?" Custer asked.

"Too long, I suppose, sir. Seventy miles, I'd guess."

Custer's fingers tapped nervously against his pistol holster. He pulled the weapon out, checking its load. "I'm going up there to the Crow's Nest and have a look myself. No more than two miles is it, Varnum?"

"About that," the lieutenant replied.

Custer glanced at his adjutant. "I'll be back in an hour, Cookey. Let's go, Varnum."

Martin expected Custer to summon him, but the general did not even look in his direction. The bugler watched him ride out with Varnum and the Crows until they vanished in a thin stand of pines along the brow of the ravine.

Martin then led his horse to a spread of grass, unfastened the bit, and let the animal graze. He realized suddenly that it was Sunday morning. He wondered if anyone else knew it was Sunday, or if they were all too tired and sleepy to care what day it was. He supposed there was no need to worry about fighting Indians for at least another day. He had heard Captain Benteen say that Monday was the day they would probably meet up with General Gibbon's soldiers and surround the Indian camp.

It seemed to Martin that Custer was gone a long time. He could tell from the sun that it was almost noon. Reaching into his haversack, he pulled out a broken piece of hardtack and began nibbling. He heard horses coming then, through the line of pines. A few stones rolled down, and a large bird flew up and sailed over the rim of the ravine.

Custer came galloping, far ahead of Varnum. His face was very red and his blue eyes were flashing like Garibaldi's. "Trumpeter Martin! Sound 'officers' call'!"

Martin grabbed at his bugle. He pulled it up to his lips, then paused a moment, his eyes questioning the command.

"Sound the call!" Custer cried. The notes rang out, urgent, blasting the silence of midday, echoing from the walls of the ravine.

"The hostiles know we're here," Custer explained to Cooke. "We found fresh pony tracks just over the ridge, and a few minutes ago saw several warriors racing for the Little Big Horn."

"That changes our plans, doesn't it, sir?"

"Of course. We'll have to attack them today instead of waiting until tomorrow for Gibbon's support."

The troop commanders were assembling hurriedly, alarmed by the surprise bugle call. While Custer explained the situation, Martin stood nearby, pretending not to listen, wondering if it was true that they must, after all, fight the Indians on Sunday.

"If we delay," Custer was explaining rapidly, "Sitting Bull will send his warriors scattering. We'll be out here into the winter searching them down. Let's finish the work now, and go back to Fort Lincoln."

"Yes, sir!" Captain Keogh replied, and most of the other officers nodded their heads in agreement.

"For the attack, we'll form in battalions. Major Reno will

take A, G and M Troops. Captain Benteen, D, H and K. Captain McDougall's B Troop will keep to the rear and guard the collected pack trains. C, E, F, I and L will be under my direct command. Gentlemen, inspect your troops for action, and march out as you are ready."

In a few minutes Trumpeter Martin was riding again, a few paces behind Custer. Soon they had climbed to the high point of the divide between the Rosebud and Little Big Horn. To the west, the country rolled for miles, with lines of low hills like ribbons of green and gray. "Over to the northwest." Custer was pointing. "That light-blue cloud. Smoke from cooking fires. Our game is near. What time is it, Cookey?"

Adjutant Cooke glanced at his watch. "Fifteen minutes past noon, sir."

Custer pulled his horse aside, waiting for Benteen, who was a few yards in the rear. "This is where you leave us, Benteen. See that line of bluffs about two miles off? Angle in that direction. Pitch into anything you come across, but notify me at once if you do."

Benteen lifted his hat in salute. "Four's left—column half right. March!" Martin watched proudly as his comrades of H Troop rode by. It was a great day for H Troop, he thought. Their bugler was riding with Custer, and they were given first position for the fighting.

As the last of Benteen's 125 men trotted away, Major Reno came up at the head of his battalion. Custer spurred his horse over to his side. "Small creek just ahead," Custer said hurriedly. "We'll follow it down to the Little Big Horn. You take the left bank, I'll take the right."

From habit, Martin's horse had wheeled to follow Custer's mount. The bugler pulled hard on the reins. His horse reared back, dancing a little so that when it came under control the young rider found himself facing the thick-necked, square-jawed Major Marcus Reno.

10

Major Marcus Reno

"That horse has spirit," Reno said.

"Pardon sir." Trumpeter Martin gathered his reins and moved out of the way.

"Forward!" Reno cried, and started his battalion moving in a slow, steady trot.

As he rode along under the hot noon sun Reno thought of the future and of the past. Before the day ended, there would probably be some fighting, although Custer seemed to believe that the hostiles would be more likely to run away. Reno remembered hard battles he had survived in the Civil War—Gaines' Mill, Malvern Hill, Antietam, Kelly's Ford, Cold Harbor, Cedar Creek. There were many more, and he had the scars of old wounds to prove it.

But he had never fought Indians. Everyone said there was no comparison between Civil War fighting and Indian fighting. Indians did not stand and fight. They were tricky—hitting and running, taking cover, hitting and running, along opposite sides of the narrow creek.

Sometimes Reno could hear Custer's voice as the general talked with his adjutant or gave orders to the scouts who were continually racing forward and returning to report. About two o'clock, a thin curl of smoke spun skyward a few hundred yards ahead. At first Reno thought it was a signal. Then as he came over a rise he saw a tepee blazing.

Custer also had seen the fire, and was splashing across the creek. Reno held his steady pace, and when he reached the burning tepee, the Rees were gathered around, looking at a dead Sioux warrior who lay inside it.

Before Reno could move closer to join Custer, one of the flankers on a nearby ridge started down at full gallop, waving his hat toward the northwest.

Reno glanced in that direction and saw a dun-colored dust cloud rising three or four miles off.

"There go your Indians!" the rider shouted. "Running like devils!"

"You're sure?" Custer cried.

"Driving in their pony herd. Big village just across the river bend!"

"Major Reno!" Custer called, beckoning with his hand. Reno spurred his horse across the sandy ground.

"Take your battalion and try to bring them to battle," Custer ordered curtly. "Charge the village. I will support you."

Reno raised his hand in a loose salute and turned his horse about. He wondered why the Rees had set the abandoned tepee on fire.

"Reno!" Custer shouted. "Take Varnum, Reynolds and the Rees. I'll keep Boyer and the Crows."

"Yes, sir." Reno motioned to Varnum to form the scouts on the left, and started his three troops moving at a trot toward the Little Big Horn. "At a gallop!" he shouted, and hoofs thundered on the hard-baked earth. In alternate trots and gallops, he took his battalion in a column of four's along a well-marked Indian trail. Ahead, the dust cloud spread and rose higher.

Suddenly the river lay in front of him, shining, running

full. "By two's! March!" Reno commanded. Harness metal rattled as gaits were quickly changed and the column broke to enter the swift-running ford. As soon as he was across the thirty-foot width of the Little Big Horn, Reno pulled his dripping horse aside. In a moment Captain French joined him.

"The horses haven't watered since last night," French shouted. "Shall we let them drink?"

"Let them get what they can as they come across," Reno answered. He glanced again toward the northwest. The dust cloud was still rising. "Close it up, close it up!" he shouted to straggling lines of troopers in the river. Some of the men were bending from their saddles, filling canteens.

Captain Moylan splashed ashore, sweat pouring off his ruddy face. "Form four's alongside Captain French's troop," Reno told him. "We'll ride down in three columns and then form a lone front for a charge into the enemy camp."

In ten minutes the troops were ready—M on the left, A in center, G on the right. Reno started them in a brisk trot, but the going was difficult over sandy ground full of wild sage, the surface chopped by pony hoofs. The Little Big Horn lay on their right now, bending like a snake, screened by tall cottonwoods and thick underbrush. On the left, a line of low hills blocked them from any possible view of Benteen's column.

The valley down which they were trotting began to widen. Reno could see the base of the moving dust cloud now, and along its fringes the fleeing hostiles—a hundred or more—driving their pony herd in toward the tepee village.

"Front into line!" he shouted, and the well-drilled troopers performed the maneuver smoothly, obliquing and spreading out in a line front across the widening valley. Troop A formed the right wing, Troop M the left. Reno signaled Varnum to move his scouts to the far left, and ordered Lieutenant Donald McIntosh to slow G Troop's pace and keep in the rear as a rallying point.

"At a gallop!" Reno cried. He spurred his horse twenty yards to front and center, and lashed the animal into a burst of speed. He could not recall ever having ridden so fast, and the men were holding to his pace. The Indians were in plain view, now, except for small dust screens which the rear riders were deliberately kicking up by circling their ponies. Suddenly the clouds lifted for a moment and Reno saw a mass of Indians, sun glinting on their rifles—far more than a hundred.

Slowing his horse, he fell back beside Moylan. Troop G was a hundred yards in the rear. He signaled Lieutenant McIntosh to bring the troop forward at a gallop and take the left side of the skirmish line.

During this slackening of pace, a large band of Sioux darted forward, firing a few shots. But as soon as Reno widened his line and started his troops galloping again, the hostiles circled back, throwing up another dust screen, whooping and yelling.

In response to the Indian yells, the charging troopers broke into cheers. Reno looked back. His men had their carbines advanced, ready for action.

Glancing forward again through a haze of dust and powder smoke, he could see the tepee village stretching along the river flats. It must be a trap, he thought. The very earth seems to grow Indians. And they are not running away. Three hundred yards to his front, they were pouring out of a ravine, waving rifles above their heads. On his left, several bands of mounted warriors were circling to get at flanks and rear.

He could feel his heart beating high. He blinked his eyes against the stinging dust, his ears straining to hear above the clatter of hoofs. A rattle of rifle fire and a whine of bullets broke the straight order of the charging line. A few horses must have been grazed by the hostile fire. Two or three reared, almost throwing their riders. The panic spread to others, and the men had trouble holding them. Suddenly one horse whinnied, then charged wildly out of M Troop, snapping its bridle rein, carrying its careening rider straight toward the Indians.

Reno knew he must make a quick decision—either turn about and dash back over the ground he had just covered, or dismount and fight on foot. "Dismount!" he cried, reining up his lathered horse. "Prepare to fight on foot!" He leaped out of the saddle, tossing his reins to his orderly. The troop commanders took up the call, sergeants echoing orders. Horse holders quickly gathered mounts and hurried them across fifty yards of open ground to a grove of timber along the river.

With the horse holders out of action, Reno quickly estimated that he had no more than ninety men on the skirmish line. He shouted orders to them to spread out. "Five-yard intervals! Five-yard intervals!"

The runaway horse had gone through the Indians, and the last Reno saw of the doomed trooper was his hatless head bobbing as horse and rider vanished among the tepees.

Carbines were crackling now, the Indians answering with individual rifle fire. "Forward, forward, steady now!" Reno ran along the rear of the advancing line, shouting orders to the men, occasionally stopping to fire his carbine. Captain French marched calmly in the center of A Troop's line, firing steadily. He paused to reload. "Winchesters!" he cried to Reno, above the din. "Too many blasted redskins armed with new Winchesters."

"Your men are firing too fast," Reno shouted back, and strode on down the line, ordering the men to fire only when a target was in their sights. He saw that some of them were already having trouble extracting empty cartridges from overheated carbines.

"Sir!" Sergeant Ryan stepped back from the line.

"Yes, Sergeant?"

"My men are running short of ammunition."

Reno guessed it would be the same all along the skirmish front. "Alternate troopers fall out and get ammunition from the saddlebags!" He pulled two men out of the line and sent them racing to the troop commanders with the order.

This sudden lessening of fire from the skirmishers encouraged the Sioux to dart in closer. One trooper fell back, wounded in the leg. Here and there men were beginning to bunch up. Reno cupped his hands. "Spread out! Spread out!" he yelled hoarsely.

He was down near the left end of the line now, where the scouts should be, but only Varnum and Reynolds were there, both kneeling and firing. "Where are the Rees?" he shouted.

"They've skedaddled," Varnum replied.

Reynolds squeezed off a shot. "No," he said. "They've taken cover, Major. They're Indians and fight like Indians."

A volley sounded from the rear, and when Reno swung around he saw blue powder smoke drifting from the woods where the horse holders were.

Reynolds also noticed it. "Some of them mounted warriors got in our rear, Major. They're threatening our horse herd."

Another volley sounded from the woods, followed by war cries and answering yells from the troopers there. Again Reno had to make a quick decision. Reynolds had said the Rees fought Indians like Indians—from concealment. The woods offered concealment. Without hesitation, he ordered Lieutenant McIntosh to withdraw G Troop from the line and move into the woods.

Meanwhile, A and M spread out to hold the skirmish position. Once again the Indians charged forward, and Reno saw men dropping out with wounds.

"We're too thin!" Moylan shouted. "They'll cut us to pieces, Major!"

"Flank to the right," Reno replied, "and fall back on the timber!"

Reno was breathing hard when the last trooper took cover in the trees. They had brought in all the wounded, and as soon as a defensive line was formed within the woods, he summoned his officers for a hasty council of war.

Just inside the first belt of cottonwoods and underbrush was a natural clearing where the horses had gathered, and Reno was surprised to find Bloody Knife, Foolish Bear and some others of the Rees there. "The scouts did good work, Major," Reynolds told him. "They helped the horse holders drive out that bunch of Sioux horse thieves."

Reno nodded. "Send two of them back to Custer," he ordered. "Tell him we're cut off here."

Reynolds translated for Bloody Knife, but the Indian shook his head. He held his hands out, opening and closing his fingers rapidly. "He says there are too many. No man could get through."

"General Custer is no longer in our rear," Captain Moylan declared. "Lieutenant De Rudio just told me he saw him on the bluffs across the river."

Reno's face revealed his concern. "Was De Rudio positive it was Custer he saw?"

"He said Cooke was with him, that they waved their hats and rode off to the north."

"I don't understand it." Reno's voice was almost a whisper. "Unless he means to attack the other side of the tepee camp."

"If Custer does that," Reynolds said, "he may find himself in the same fix we're in."

A scattering of carbine fire broke out suddenly, and sergeants began calling orders. "Look to that, McIntosh," Reno said. "It's on your front." He took his field glass and scanned the line of low bluffs east of the river.

On the far left of his field of vision he picked up a single horseman—an Indian wearing a buckskin shirt. Reno's heart missed a beat. Perhaps it is my imagination, he thought. He sharpened the focus. He has the look of a general directing a battle. Could it be Sitting Bull?

He cased the field glass, blinked his eyes, and saw Surgeon DeWolf approaching. "What are our casualties, Surgeon?" he called.

"One man dead. Several wounded," DeWolf replied. "Dr. Porter wants to know how long we'll be here. One man needs surgery."

"We could hold out here for awhile," Reno said, as if talking to himself.

"Our ammunition won't last till dark," French warned him.

"And if we remain here, we can't rejoin Custer," Reno admitted. "Nor can he likely relieve us, hidden here as we are in the woods." He glanced at the bluffs again. "Our best chance seems to be a dash for one of those hills. Custer could see us there, and perhaps we could see him. Is it agreed?"

"You are in command," French said.

Reno looked at Bloody Knife, then said to Reynolds: "Ask him if he can lead us across the river to the high ground." Reynolds translated, and Bloody Knife nodded, muttering a few words deep in his throat.

"He says some of us will die," Reynolds explained quickly, "but that some of us will live to get there if we ride very fast."

Carbines began popping along the semicircular defense line. "They're coming in!" a trooper yelled. A moment later a volley roared from the woods.

"That's my troop!" French cried, and started off on the run.

"Withdraw your men to this clearing," Reno shouted after him. "And mount up by four's for a charge!" He turned to his orderly and told him to bring their horses.

As soon as Reno was mounted, he circled the clearing,

directing preparations for the charge. At first there was little difficulty, but when the attacking Sioux saw what was happening they pressed into the woods. While the troopers were mounting, a determined band of warriors rushed the clearing. Bullets whined from their Winchesters. One man in M Troop toppled from his horse. Two of his comrades, still dismounted, pulled him into the brush.

Reno wheeled his horse beside Bloody Knife, motioning with his hand to move out. A second later Bloody Knife fell back in his saddle, as if jerked by a rope. A bullet had torn its way into his forehead, spattering blood across Reno's sleeve. The Indian's horse spun around, throwing its dead rider to the ground.

"For'ard!" Reno shouted.

As he led the way in a tearing gallop out of the woods he looked back over his shoulder. Troop A was coming along in good formation, Moylan at the head. On the far, high horizon, the lone Indian horseman still sat watching the valley. He must be, Reno thought, none other than that crafty old medicine chief of the Hunkpapa Sioux—Sitting Bull.

11

Sitting Bull

June 25, 6 A.M.–4 P.M.

On the morning of June 25, Sitting Bull sat cross-legged in front of his tepee, warming himself in the sun. It was a lazy day with only a little wind, and soon the sun would be hot. Along the flats he could see most of the Hunkpapa Sioux camp, smoke curling from tepee holes. Children played in the sand along the Little Big Horn, and some young men were fishing there. A few yards to his right, his wife Pretty Plume was scraping a buffalo skin. She was humming quietly to herself.

Sitting Bull stretched himself and reached for a leather-covered book which he had found on the battlefield after the Sioux and Cheyennes had whipped the soldier-chief Three Stars, the one the white men called Crook. They had given General Crook a good beating and sent him and his soldiers limping back to the south.

The leather-covered book had leaves filled with strange marks which the white men called writing, but some of the pages were blank. He meant to use them for drawing picture stories. He wondered why the white men did not make pictures instead of tiny scratches to tell their stories.

Thinking of the picture stories reminded him of the fine pictograph on deerskin he had lost during the Sun Dance. Someday when he was passing the place where the Sioux held their Sun Dance along the Rosebud, he would stop and search for it. He had been too excited at the time to notice its loss, because during the Sun Dance he had seen the greatest vision of his life.

Each day for an hour or more since the vision had come to him, he had sat and recalled it in detail, even the chant which had come to him from the Sun:

> Now he is walking
> Now he is walking
> This is a buffalo bull walking.

He remembered dancing all one day, facing the sun from the time of its rising to the time of its setting. And then he had danced all night and until noon of the next day, when he fainted and fell down and dreamed the great vision. The warriors later told him they threw cold water on him for a long time before he awoke from the dreaming.

Everyone in the Sun Dance Lodge was eager to hear of his vision. He told them of the chant he had heard from the Sun, and then a voice crying: "I give you these because they have no ears." He had looked up, in the dream, and saw many blue-coated soldiers falling from the sky like grasshoppers, with their heads down and their hats falling off. They were falling right into the Indian camp.

He did not have to explain the vision to his people. They knew that many soldiers would soon be coming to their camp. They knew the soldiers would be coming upside down, which meant they would be killed. There was no need for any more sun dancing. They must prepare now for the fighting.

News of Sitting Bull's vision spread like a grass fire across the prairie. Gall, the war chief of the Hunkpapas, came every day to Sitting Bull's tepee to talk of the soldiers falling into camp. Crazy Horse, mighty chief of the Oglalla Sioux, and Two Moons of the Cheyenne also came there. Sitting Bull told them the tribes should all stay together so that they could help one another when the soldiers came.

Crazy Horse agreed. He said the Indians must learn to fight like the bluecoat soldiers. They should stay together and throw all their arrows and bullets at once into the enemy, instead of every warrior fighting for himself. And they should also send out scouts, as the soldiers did. "Sitting Bull's vision has told us the soldiers are coming," Crazy Horse said, "but we do not know from which of the four directions they will come. We must send out scouts so we will know where the soldiers are."

"Our runners told us that Long Hair Custer came to Powder River," Sitting Bull replied. "But he has gone away from us—north to the Yellowstone."

"Long Hair Custer may come back this way. And there may be other soldiers," Crazy Horse insisted. "We should send some of our young men in all the directions, to look for them."

Sitting Bull smoked his pipe and thought for awhile. "Crazy Horse has spoken well," he said. "We will send scouts to look out for the soldiers."

This was how the chiefs learned that Three Stars Crook was coming. Far to the south where the Rosebud was only a trickling branch of water, some of the scouts sighted Crook's column. There were many bluecoats—pony soldiers and walking soldiers.

At first, Sitting Bull wanted to wait for these invaders to fall into camp. But the young braves were eager to go and fight them, and he knew that if he waited too long, many of the warriors would go off in the old way, fighting in small war parties, killing a few stragglers, stealing a few horses. By the time Three Stars found the camp, there might not be enough warriors there to defend it.

So Sitting Bull and Crazy Horse called together a great war party. They rode swiftly in the night up into the headwaters of the Rosebud. There they found Crook's camp, and attacked it at daybreak in the same way soldiers so often attacked Indian camps. It was a bitter fight that lasted all day, but before sundown the soldiers knew they were whipped. Crook ordered a retreat.

Sitting Bull was pleased by the victory, but was sad because eleven of his best warriors were dead. He knew also that there must be another fight soon. His vision of soldiers falling into camp had not yet come to pass.

After the battle, he persuaded all the chiefs and subchiefs to follow him down to this new camp on the Little Big Horn. They would stay there during the Moon When the Ponies Get Fat. Grass and wood were plentiful, buffalo herds were nearby, there were fish in the river. The men wounded in the fight with Crook could heal themselves. The warriors could clean their guns and sharpen their knives, reload and recap their empty cartridge shells.

Every day now warriors were coming in from faraway reservations to join the new camp. They had heard of Sitting Bull's vision, and wanted to be in the camp where the soldiers would come falling upside down. They told Sitting Bull they were tired of living penned up like animals on reservations ruled by the White Father's agents. They did not like to eat stringy beef spoiled so badly that even a dog could not swallow it. They wanted to be free like the wind, free to hunt buffalo, to live again in the free country of their forefathers.

As he sat before his tepee in the warming sunlight on the morning of June 25, Sitting Bull thought of all these things. Bobtail Horse, a Cheyenne runner, had come to him two days ago with news that Long Hair Custer and many soldiers were marching up the Rosebud. Perhaps Custer was going to help Three Stars Crook. If Custer followed the Rosebud, he would not find the camp on the Little Big

Horn. Perhaps it was just as well. But soon, Sitting Bull knew, some soldiers must come to this camp.

He gazed at the forest of tepees circling along the flats. These were only the Hunkpapa lodges. Around the river bend were Minneconjous and Oglallas, and still farther along was the Cheyenne camp. All together there were 4,000 warriors—more than half of them armed with rifles, some with new Winchesters. For many moons, everybody had worked hard to collect all these things. The women had dressed thousands of buffalo robes to trade for guns and ammunition. The warriors had risked their lives to take horses from miners and soldiers.

These were the last real Indians, Sitting Bull thought. These were not trading-post beggars willing to swap their hunting grounds and their freedom for a small corner of a reservation. They were strong enough now to show the White Father's soldiers that they could not be driven upon reservations. Perhaps the soldiers would soon learn to leave them alone. It would be good to live in peace again and not be hunted like wild animals.

The sun was growing too warm. He decided to walk over to the council tepee in the middle of the camp and learn the news of the day. Rising, he brushed dust from leggings and moccasins, straightened his braids over his chest, and set a single eagle feather at the back of his head. He was a big man with a stern face, and as he walked along he limped slightly, favoring an old wound in his left hip.

Gall, the warrior chief, and a number of subchiefs were seated in the shade at one side of the council tepee. They were talking of going on a buffalo hunt. After greeting Sitting Bull with courtesy, they made a place for him in the circle. The conversation resumed, and Sitting Bull was about to speak when a young warrior came dashing up on a pony.

"Soldiers!" the young man cried. "Long Hair Custer has come from the Rosebud!"

Sitting Bull and Gall both sprang to their feet. Upriver a cloud of dust towered in the sky. The herder boys were bringing in the ponies. And beyond the first dust was another one, boiling along over the treetops—the soldiers!

"Gather your warriors," Sitting Bull said calmly to Gall. "The soldiers are falling into camp."

Gall took a pistol from his belt and fired into the air. His head was thrown back, his broad face defiant. "Today we will show them what fighters we are!" he cried, and leaped on his pony. Sitting Bull watched him race through the camp, summoning the warriors, then he hurried back to his tepee.

Pretty Plume was already bringing the horses. "Ride far out on the prairie," Sitting Bull told her. "Help the other women, the old ones and the ones with little children." He ran into the tepee, buckled on his cartridge belt, and armed himself with a shield, a revolver and his prized Winchester rifle.

When he came outside, a stream of women and children was moving down the flats, turning leftward to make room for the warriors galloping up from the Oglalla camp. He saw Crazy Horse coming along in front on his yellow pinto.

Mounting quickly, Sitting Bull lashed his horse with a quirt until the animal was flying through the camp. He met the pony herd racing in. Warriors on foot were dashing alongside, desperately seeking mounts. Some would grasp at a shaggy mane, leap upon a pony's back, and quickly turn toward the oncoming enemy. Others swung lariats to catch a steed.

Gall was gathering warriors around him in a shallow ravine, sending out small war parties on foot to delay the soldiers. As soon as enough mounted warriors assembled, he sent them circling to get at the soldiers' rear.

Dust was so thick that Sitting Bull could catch only brief glimpses of the soldiers. The first time he saw them they were charging very fast; the next time they had slowed

down. The soldier-chief was not Long Hair Custer. He had
pulled his horse back into the line and was waving his arms
and shouting.

Suddenly one of the soldiers came dashing straight toward Sitting Bull. For a moment the chief thought the bluecoat must be leading a charge. Then he saw that the
soldier's bridle rein was broken. Gall's warriors opened to
avoid being trampled, and horse and rider shot past them
into the tepees, several braves in pursuit.

Now all at once the soldiers were dismounting, and a
rattle of carbines ripped across the irregular rifle fire of
Gall's warriors. "Warriors!" Sitting Bull cried, "we have everything to fight for, and if we are defeated we shall have
nothing to live for, so let us fight like brave men!"

He held his horse steady. Powder smoke filled his nostrils,
and the din of gunfire, yells and commands deafened his
ears. There was something strange about the action of the
soldiers, slowing their charge and then dismounting. Why
would they do such a foolish thing? Unless there were other
soldiers, somewhere else. The soldier-chief out there must be
waiting for Custer to come and help him!

It could be a trick, Sitting Bull thought, and quickly
swung his horse around and started on a trot for the nearest
hill across the river. He splashed through the swift waters of
the Little Big Horn, and in a minute or so he could look
down upon the soldiers who were not retreating into a
thicket. He glanced southward where the other soldiers
must be, but nothing moved there.

He could see Gall in the valley, directing the encirclement
of the woods where the soldiers were. It was not a good
place for a fight. The soldiers could stay there all day, killing
some of the bravest warriors. But Gall was a strong war
chief and would not let his warriors throw their lives away
for nothing.

In a little open space in the woods, some soldiers were
mounting their horses. Perhaps a messenger had come to

them from the other soldiers, from Long Hair Custer. Were they going to charge the camp now? A volley of rifle fire echoed against the hills. Sitting Bull raised his quirt, but let it down softly. The soldiers were charging out of the woods, but they were going away from the camp. They were running away! The soldier-chief's horse was jumping like a rabbit, with frightened bluecoats strung out behind him like wild geese in flight.

Sitting Bull reached for the field glass he had taken from a dead soldier long ago down on Tongue River. He fixed it on the fleeing soldiers. They were so frightened they were running away and leaving their wounded in the woods. He could also see some soldiers who had lost their horses. They were trying to hide from Gall's warriors there in the thickets.

Racing along one dusty flank of the soldiers was Crazy Horse and a band of Oglallas, firing broadside as they galloped. It was like a buffalo hunt. A thousand warriors chasing a hundred soldiers. But Sitting Bull knew they were wasting many bullets in the excitement of the chase. The dust was too thick for good shooting.

Now the soldier-chief was plunging his horse into the river. He had lost his hat—like the soldiers in the vision. Behind him, bluecoats were bunching along the river bank. The place was not a good place to cross, because horses had to jump down into the water. Some would hesitate, and the riders behind were running right into them. They made good targets for the pursuing Sioux.

But in a few minutes the surviving soldiers were all across and scrambling up a claybank to the top of a bluff. They had to dismount and lead their horses. A few Sioux followed them, but the soldiers had the advantage now, and could fire down on their pursuers.

"Let them go," Sitting Bull muttered aloud. "Let a few of them live to remember how badly they were beaten."

He shifted his glass back to the woods where a few warriors were still searching for soldiers left behind. Down there he saw a movement behind a bush, and then a face showed clearly—an Indian face. But this Indian was not a Sioux. He was a Corn Indian, an Arickaree, one of the soldiers' scouts hired to track down the Sioux. Sitting Bull spat in disgust. He would like to go down and count *coup* on that one himself. What a pity that old tribal enemies could not make peace and join together, instead of hiring out to the soldiers!

Ay-ee! He sighed. His vision had come true. Soldiers had fallen upside down into his camp. But there were not as many soldiers as he had dreamed. No. Where was Long Hair Custer? He turned his horse in a complete circle, and then off to the northwest he saw a thin trail of dust. There they were, running away from the fighting. Or were they? If they turned toward the sun, they would come down to the river just across from where the Cheyennes were camped. He had better send a warning by some of the Cheyennes who had come to help the Hunkpapas.

He turned about and took one more look through his field glass at the woods. He saw the Arickaree again, creeping along the brushy bank of the river, trying to catch a loose pony. The Ree was so clumsy in his movements that he frightened the grazing animal away. He had none of the grace of a stalking Sioux, in fact he reminded Sitting Bull of a foolish bear.

12

Foolish Bear

June 25, 3 P.M.–4 P.M.

When Major Reno ordered his troopers to fight on foot, Foolish Bear was one of the Rees who went into the woods with the horse holders. He led his own horse and three others.

Foolish Bear was pleased to be in the cover of the woods. He felt much braver there. He did not understand why the soldiers liked to be out in the open to do their fighting, especially when they were outnumbered by so many Sioux. The sensible thing, he thought, was to take cover and make the Sioux risk their lives to find them.

Even though he felt braver in the woods, Foolish Bear was sure the soldiers were going to be beaten. If the soldiers were defeated, the Rees would be defeated too. And because the Sioux hated the Rees even more than the soldiers, the Rees would have to be very crafty indeed to live to see another sun come out of its rising place.

The horse holders had not been in the woods long when they heard noises in the brush below them. A rifle fired, and then another, and one of the troopers yelled "Indians!" They tied their horses to some trees, and formed a line in the clearing and began firing carbines into the woods. Foolish Bear did not join the line. He circled around through the brush until he saw a Sioux warrior very close. Foolish Bear fired at him. The Sioux did not utter a word, but clapped a hand against one leg and hopped away through the bushes to where he had left his horse. Foolish Bear shot at him again, but the Sioux rode swiftly away.

After that there was no more trouble for a few minutes, and then Major Reno brought all his soldiers into the woods. But for some reason, Major Reno did not want to stay and fight there. All at once he ordered his men to mount up. Foolish Bear went looking for the four horses he had tied to a tree, but in all the confusion some others had taken them. He began running all around searching for them, and when he saw Bloody Knife he started toward him to tell him about the horses.

He had not taken three steps when a party of Sioux charged out of the brush and fired a volley. A soldier fell out of his saddle. Then Bloody Knife's horse jumped, and Bloody Knife fell dead on the ground.

Foolish Bear did not know what to do then. Major Reno and the mounted soldiers went galloping out of the clearing, and soldiers on foot were running about looking for horses. It was a bad sign indeed that the Sioux had killed Bloody Knife. No others of the scouts had such strong medicine as Bloody Knife, who had been carrying a bear's claw with a clam shell on it and a black handkerchief with blue stars that Custer had given him.

He ran into the thickest part of the brush and a few yards away saw Surgeon DeWolf and three soldiers helping the wounded man who had been shot off his horse. They had four horses with them. Foolish Bear decided that this must be the time for him to give back to Surgeon DeWolf the tooth he had pulled.

From inside his shirt, Foolish Bear took a rawhide pouch filled with powdered charcoal. He shook out a small blue

feather to which he had fastened his tooth with a wrapping
of horse hairs. He was sure that it possessed magic powers,
because Surgeon DeWolf had driven evil spirits from it.
Thus far it had protected Foolish Bear from the Sioux, and
if he explained this to Surgeon DeWolf and gave it to him,
perhaps the soldier medicine man would let him ride behind
his saddle.

Just as he started toward the group, Surgeon DeWolf
reached for the bridle rein of his horse and mounted. "He
can't live with that stomach wound," the surgeon said.
"You'd better mount up, boys, and ride out of here."

"I'll leave him my canteen," one of the soldiers said, and
then they all jumped on their horses and started through the
woods toward the river.

"Wait! wait!" Foolish Bear called in Arickaree, making
the sign with his right hand and holding the feathered tooth
in his left. One of the soldiers jerked his carbine around and
was about to shoot, but another one cried: "It's one of the
Ree scouts." They trotted out of sight through the trees.

Now Foolish Bear was all alone, but all through the
woods he could hear stealthy movements of both friends and
enemies and occasional firing. To the south, there was constant firing, and he knew that those riding with Major Reno
were having a bad time.

He fastened the feathered tooth in his scalp lock and decided to search for a horse along the river bank. Underbrush
grew very close there, and most of the time he crawled
along, listening carefully. He could hear water running in
the river, and a bell tinkled softly. He peered out and saw a
black pony. A tiny bell hung from a buckskin around its
neck. It bore Sioux markings—red paint slapped on one
haunch by an open hand.

Foolish Bear tried desperately to catch the horse, but it
kept moving away. Finally he leaped out, waving his arms,
and the horse plunged into the river. Foolish Bear dived in
behind, and as the current carried them along he managed

to get a good grip on the pony's mane. He pulled the bell off and rode out into a thin stand of cottonwoods. Upstream he could see Major Reno's soldiers climbing a bluff. A small band of mounted Sioux was circling around to their left.

Then he saw Surgeon DeWolf and the three soldiers going up a ravine just below where the Sioux were. He wanted to shout to them and warn them of the Sioux, but the distance was too great. In a minute or so, the Sioux sighted the four riders and began firing down at them. Two of the soldiers escaped by galloping to the right, but Surgeon DeWolf and the other one fell down on the ground, their horses running away, with the Sioux after them.

For awhile Foolish Bear held the black pony behind a low-hanging cottonwood limb, looking out through the leaves. He felt pity for Surgeon DeWolf, because he lay quite still and was surely dead. After awhile Foolish Bear took the feathered tooth from his scalp lock and threw it upon the ground. Its magic power was gone.

He heard a splashing in the river and saw five or six soldiers swimming hard for the bank. They were holding up their carbines to keep them dry. A Sioux was coming along to head them off. The hoofs of his pony made sucking noises as it stepped high in the muddy footing. The lower half of the Sioux warrior's face was painted red, the upper half yellow.

Foolish Bear fired at him, but the bullets only frightened the pony. By this time the soldiers were out of the water, and the Sioux took cover in the woods.

On top of the bluff a flag was flying now, and the soldiers up there were firing so hard that most of their Sioux pursuers had retreated across the river. Foolish Bear decided to try to make a run for it, all the way up the slope to the flag.

He nudged the black pony out of the woods, slapped it hard with his open hand, and lay flat on its back, clinging to its mane. The soldiers who had swum the river thought he was a Sioux, and fired a shot or two at him. He looked back at them, shouting: "Ree! Ree!" He recognized the big soldier in front, the one they called Fritz—Trooper John Sivertsen.

13

Trooper John Sivertsen

June 25, 3 P.M.–4 P.M.

When Major Reno gave the order to take cover, M Troop was far over to the left of the valley. The command was "Retreat to the timber," but Captain French insisted that his troopers keep their faces to the enemy.

John Sivertsen would have given anything to have his horse right then. He thought he would never make it into the woods. He heard Captain French yell, "Flank to the right," and then a minute later Sergeant Ryan bellowed, "Left face!" Sivertsen was Number One in his set of four's, but he held himself hunched forward and kept squeezing the trigger of his carbine and reloading. The Sioux were coming up on foot thick as ants. He thought the line would never cross that last open space. Two men in his platoon went down, but they weren't hurt so badly they couldn't scramble into the brush.

Once they were in the woods, Captain French lined them up behind some trees, and the Sioux scattered off the front so there were not many targets for a little while.

Ryan came along the platoon line, slapping his boys on the back. "Big Fritz!" he cried when he saw Sivertsen. "If the redskins couldn't hit a target like you, they're no match for M Troop. I say let's go after 'em!"

Sivertsen was still breathing hard. "You go first, Ryan," he retorted, and dried his sweating palms on his trousers.

"Just as soon as Major Reno gives the word," Ryan declared, and went on to the next trooper.

The break in the firing lasted only a minute or so. The Sioux worked their way around to the flanks and then into the woods, and soon their rifle fire was growing steadily hotter. Bullets were clipping leaves off trees, and men were beginning to go down all around Sivertsen. He was bothered because no matter which way he turned he could see no Indians. He could hear them signaling with their bone whistles, and they seemed to be on all sides.

Somewhere in the rear Captain French's voice was barking commands, but the banging of gunfire never let up long enough for Sivertsen to understand what the captain was shouting. Not long after that he heard a volley of rifle fire, yells and a rumble of hoofbeats. He could see nothing through the brush behind him, but heard one of the M Troop boys cry: "They're charging out! Let's go get our horses."

Sivertsen hurried along with the others through the woods to the edge of a clearing. He saw a dozen troopers go galloping away, pursued by several Indians on foot.

In the clearing lay Bloody Knife and a dead trooper. The only horse in sight was also dead.

"They've run out on us," somebody said.

For the first time Sivertsen looked at his companions. There were eight of them, all M Troop privates.

"We'd better stay under cover," he said, ducking back into the brush, the others following behind him.

He heard a crackling of leaves, and motioned his companions to silence, holding his carbine at ready. He had the weapon up to fire when he saw Lieutenant De Rudio move out from behind a tree.

"Lieutenant!" he called softly.

The Italian spun around, his revolver out. "Big Fritz!" he spluttered. "How many with you?"

"Eight," Sivertsen told him.

"Good. I have found four boys from G Troop."

Sivertsen recognized Tom O'Neill in the group.

De Rudio quickly checked their arms and ammunition. "We can defend ourselves," he said. "We have no horses, but I think if we go along in the woods, maybe we can cross the river to Major Reno."

Sivertsen was glad a lieutenant was present to give orders. There wasn't a noncom in the bunch, and he knew the others would have expected him to lead because he was Big Fritz.

They circled the clearing and kept in the thickets, moving in double time when they could. The rifle fire upriver was a steady roar broken by the occasional bang of a carbine. After two or three minutes, the woods cover thinned and narrowed. Out on the flats they could see their mounted comrades jammed together at the river crossing, with a scattered file strung out in the rear, every man racing for his life.

"There's Charley Reynolds!" Sivertsen cried. Across a ravine, Reynolds and a small group of soldiers were kneeling in a semicircle, pouring a steady fire into the pursuing Sioux. The scout saw De Rudio's party and shouted to them: "Come on, boys, let's try to stop these Indians while our soldiers get across!"

At De Rudio's commands, Sivertsen and the other troopers began firing volleys. Because of their distance from the rapidly moving hostiles, they scored only a few hits. Sivertsen emptied his carbine and felt along his cartridge belt. "One more load, Lieutenant," he announced quietly.

"They got Reynolds!" The cry came from across the ravine. A moment later the soldiers over there dropped down the bank and began scattering toward the river.

Sivertsen could see Reynolds' motionless form lying face

forward in the grass. A half-dozen mounted Sioux dashed up, firing across at De Rudio's men.

"Back into the woods!" the lieutenant shouted. "Scatter out!"

Sivertsen fired a farewell shot at the Sioux. He saw one of them leap off his pony near Reynolds. In the sunlight, a scalp knife flashed.

With De Rudio leading, they hurried back over the same way they had come, then turned down a dry wash toward the river. "Halt!" De Rudio's voice was husky. He held his left hand out, waving it up and down.

"That's a guidon over there, sir," Sivertsen whispered. "One of A Troop's."

"I see it." De Rudio's eyes were blinking against the yellow light sifting through the trees. "My troop's guidon," the lieutenant added.

De Rudio whistled, softly at first, then shrilly. "Anyone there?" he called. At the top of the opposite embankment, the guidon remained motionless, its staff thrust into soft earth at an angle. De Rudio turned, his dark face close to Sivertsen's. "It is my duty to recover my troop's colors," he said. "Keep me covered."

Jumping into the dry creek bed, De Rudio lunged across. His boot heels dug into the opposite bank as he reached for the leaning guidon. He caught the staff and tugged, but the cloth dragged against a bush. At the same time gunfire burst from the woods beyond, bullets whining in the foliage above Sivertsen's head.

De Rudio slid down the bank, and for a second Sivertsen thought the lieutenant had been hit. But he was on his feet again, motioning the soldiers back.

"Scatter boys," Sivertsen yelled. "Head for the river!"

The woods were full of Indians blowing their bone whistles and shooting at any sign of a blue uniform. Sivertsen kept working toward the river, and in a minute or so there it was—deep and flowing fast. He dropped down in a patch of high grass, and almost fell over a trooper.

"Fritz!" a weak voice cried. "I thought I had an Indian on me." The wounded man was Charley White, an M Troop sergeant.

"We've got to cross that river," Sivertsen said. "The woods back there are alive with Sioux looking for us." He noticed a stain of blood on Sergeant White's trouser leg. "You hurt bad, Sergeant?"

"I lost a lot of blood before I stopped it. I could never swim that river, Fritz."

Sivertsen raised up cautiously. He saw four of the M Troop boys at the edge of the woods. "Bunched together little ducks on a pond," he muttered, and waved frantically until they saw him. He beckoned them to come on.

"You willing to take orders from me, Sergeant?" he asked White.

"Anything you say, Big Fritz." The sergeant smiled faintly.

"Lieutenant De Rudio is somewhere back in there, but we've no time to wait for him." He reached for White's carbine and canteen, ordered two of the troopers to lift the sergeant, and then led the way into the river. "Boys," he said calmly. "I think I'm tall enough to wade this here Little Big Horn. One of you take hold of my collar, the rest of you hold up old Sergeant White, and we'll make it."

They were halfway across when they saw a painted warrior coming along the opposite bank on a pony. *"Uh-oh,"* Sivertsen said. "Keep your carbines dry, boys, we're going to swim out shooting."

An unexpected shot came from somewhere. The Sioux pony reared and skittered off into the woods. Sivertsen was gasping for breath. At last his boots dragged in the muddy riverbank. He turned and gave a hand to the man behind him, then helped Sergeant White limp to dry ground. Still carrying two carbines, and with one arm supporting the ser-

geant, Sivertsen started in a lumbering trot toward the distant bluff. Blue powder smoke ringed the rim, and a flag was
fluttering there in a lazy late-afternoon breeze.

"Come on, boys," Sivertsen yelled. "Double time!"

A black pony dashed across in front of them. Two troopers fired wild shots at the Indian flattened on the animal's
back.

"He's hollering about something," Sivertsen said.

"Fritz," asked Sergeant White, "is that one of our boys
down over there in that gully?"

Sivertsen squinted across the shadowed grass. He motioned to two of the troopers behind him. "Go have a look.
Might be wounded. Hurry!" He kept on at a steady jog trot,
forcing White to keep up, sometimes lifting and carrying the
sergeant.

In a minute or so the two men rejoined them. "Trooper
Eli Clare and Surgeon DeWolf," one of them said soberly.
"Both dead and scalped."

Sivertsen glanced back across the river and sucked in a
deep breath. From the point where Charley Reynolds had
been killed, all the way to the river crossing, dead men and
horses lay in an irregular line. "Clare and the surgeon are
not the only ones," he said softly. "I reckon we were lucky
after all."

The climbing was slow now as the slope steepened. Mud
and water squeezed up out of his boot tops at every step. He
could feel his slimy socks balling up around his heels.

He heard a sudden burst of cheers, and men came leaping
down the hill. Sivertsen raised his head. Captain French was
standing in front of him, reaching out a hand. "Fritz, I'm
glad to see you," the captain said hoarsely. His sunburned
face was streaked with sweat and dust. "And Sergeant
White. We counted you all dead."

"We would be, sir," White replied, "had it not been for
Big Fritz." The sergeant coughed and sank down on the
ground. "I'd like to put in a word for his promotion, sir."

The captain's eyes were fixed on the valley below. "I'll keep it in mind. Right now, you boys better take the sergeant back to Dr. Porter. There's a fire going there. All of you dry yourselves and then come forward and start digging entrenchments. The Sioux down there are massing on both our flanks for another attack."

Sivertsen helped Sergeant White to his feet and glanced down the slope. Sioux were pouring out of the woods and crossing the river. "We made it just in time," he said.

The sergeant nodded. "They would have found me in that grass for sure." Sivertsen could feel White's shoulders shivering when the wind on the summit struck his wet uniform.

A horseman came galloping along the ridge, calling for Captain French. Sivertsen had to look at the rider twice before he recognized him as Major Reno. A white handkerchief was bound around his forehead, and his eyes rolled wildly. "Captain French!" Reno shouted. "Pull your men back over the brow of the slope. There's not enough cover here to make a stand!"

"Yes, sir." French waved his troopers up the bluff.

Sivertsen led the way back to Surgeon Porter's improvised hospital—a small hollow surrounded by the battalion's picketed horses. About twenty men lay on the sandy ground, some covered with horse blankets. "Another one for you, Doctor," Sivertsen said.

Porter was wrapping a man's leg with bandages. He glanced up briefly. "Make him comfortable as you can," he replied hurriedly, and then noticed their wet uniforms. "You boys just come in?"

"Yes, sir."

"See anything of Surgeon DeWolf?"

"He's dead, sir," Sivertsen told him.

Porter shook his head, his big walrus mustaches quivering. His fingers continued to roll the bandage. "A pity. I promised his wife I'd look after him."

A small fire was blazing nearby, and Sivertsen and the four men with him sat down around it. They removed their boots and held their muddy socks over the flames until they steamed partially dry. A peppering of carbine fire sounded from the front of the bluff.

"Let's go," Sivertsen said. At least his toes felt dry inside his damp boots.

When they reached the M Troop line, the Indians had been driven away. Sergeant Ryan was directing the digging of entrenchments. "Fritz, you lucky old ox," Ryan cried. "The sight of you warms my heart!"

Sivertsen was startled by the number of Indians now assembled on both ends of the slope. They were circling their ponies and shouting insults and threats at the troopers. One of them wore a trailing war bonnet.

"Yeah, I reckon you could use a few more than me, too, Sergeant."

"We can hold 'em till Custer gets here," Ryan replied confidently. "Dig awhile, shoot awhile."

"What do I dig with? My spade was on my horse."

"You carry a knife, don't you, Fritz?"

"Sure, but I can't dig much of a hole with a knife."

"You'd better dig one," Ryan said, and took out his own knife to help.

Sivertsen chose a place behind a two-foot sagebrush, and began slicing at the hard ground, piling the earth up with his hands. Ryan dug beside him. "Make it deep and wide, Fritz. That sagebrush won't stop any bullets."

"Here they come again!" somebody shouted.

Both Sivertsen and Ryan grabbed their carbines. "Hold your fire until I give the command," the sergeant ordered the platoon.

A wave of mounted Indians fanned across the slope, shooting with rifles and bows. A bullet kicked up dust from the mound in front of Sivertsen. "Fire!" Ryan yelled. The carbine fire was like a snarl of defiance. A Sioux pony went down, and its rider ran zigzagging for cover in a ravine.

"That showed 'em," Ryan declared. "Back to your digging, boys."

Sivertsen borrowed some cartridges from Ryan, reloaded his carbine, placed it within easy reach, and resumed digging. "I noticed a bit of blood on your sleeve, Sergeant," he said. "You catch one?"

"Just a scratch on the shoulder. A big Sioux came alongside my horse as I was heading for the crossing. Tried to pull me from the saddle. He hung on till my horse started to jump in the river. Then he dropped back and let fire. Right then was when Lieutenant Benny Hodgson got it." Rayan patted a field-glass case he had slung around his neck. "This was the lieutenant's. I swung down and picked it off the grass as I rode by. Captain French told me to keep it and use it."

"We lost a lot of men in that charge, didn't we?"

"Twelve missing out of M Troop. I figure they're done for. And we took five wounded over to Dr. Porter. Lost Lieutenant Hodgson and Lieutenant McIntosh. And Surgeon DeWolf."

"Add Charley Reynolds to your list, Ryan. I saw him get it."

"No! So old Charley's luck ran out."

Sivertsen smoothed his earth embankment and stabbed steadily into the deepening pit. "Maybe we should have stayed in the woods."

Ryan had the field glass up, scanning the southwestern horizon. "Nobody will ever know, Fritz. There was an awful lot of hostiles in there." His forehead wrinkled over the glass. "Looks like dust. Maybe Custer's decided to come on. When he gets here, he'll make 'em pay."

Sivertsen grunted. "Custer's sure been taking his time."

"Here, have a look off there, Fritz. Maybe your eyes are better'n mine."

Sivertsen took the glasses in his grimy hands and adjusted the focus. "It's a column coming, for certain, Sergeant." He shifted the glass slightly to the left and picked up a lone horseman galloping madly toward the rolling dust. Two Indians were in pursuit. "Say, Ryan, have a look! If I'm not mistaken, the trooper on that horse is John Martin!"

14

Trumpeter John Martin

June 25, 2:15 P.M.–5 P.M.

As soon as Major Reno's battalion trotted away from the burning tepee, General Custer ordered John Martin to sound "boots and saddles." The five troops formed, and in a minute they were in motion. Martin rode to the right and rear of Custer.

For two hundred yards they followed Reno's dust trail, then swung right. "At a gallop!" Custer shouted to Martin, and the trumpeter turned in his saddle and blew the call. For three or four minutes the column of four's thundered along the floor of a ravine, then slowed to a trot and a walk as they approached a narrow creek.

"Water horses," Custer said.

Martin let his mount wade into the clear pebbled stream. While the horse was still drinking, Mark Kellogg came up on a gray mule.

"That mule is faster than most of my horses," Custer remarked lightly.

Kellogg lifted his boots from the stirrups, to keep them out of the creek. "Old Horace Greeley keeps a steady but sure pace," the newspaperman replied.

"From now on," Custer warned, "Horace will have to go some to keep up. In another few minutes, we'll be charging the other end of that hostile camp."

"Horace and I don't mind in the slightest, observing the action from the rear." Kellogg took a notebook and pencil from his pocket and began sketching the hills on their left.

"Don't straggle, Mark," Custer said seriously. "When we go in, we'll stir up a lot of wild bucks who'll be circling on our flanks and rear."

After march was resumed, Kellogg and his mule Horace Greeley rode alongside Trumpeter Martin. But as soon as the rear of the column crossed the creek, Custer ordered a gallop. The short-legged mule could not keep abreast. Kellogg pulled out to one side, waving gaily. "Remember the tortoise and the hare!" he shouted after Custer.

"Take care!" the general replied. They were approaching a big hill that overlooked the river valley on their left. Custer signaled a turn to the right, continuing in a fast trot for four or five hundred yards around the base. Then he called a sudden halt.

Dust swirled over Trumpeter Martin. His horse was breathing hard and was blowing froth from around its mouth bit.

Custer squinted at the sun over the hill, then beckoned to Martin to follow him. Straight up the steep slope the general and the trumpeter climbed, saddle leather creaking when their mounts lunged over gullies.

At the top Custer pulled up, standing in the stirrups. Martin came alongside. His horse was snuffling for air. In the valley below, a tremendous Indian village curled along the river.

"Not a warrior in sight," Custer declared. "They must be asleep in their tepees." He lifted his field glass and scanned the valley.

In the village, Martin could see children playing, some squaws at work, and a few dogs and ponies.

"Reno must be taking his time fording the river," Custer said half aloud.

"A dust cloud is rising over to the south, sir," Martin told him.

"Yes." Custer cased his glass, his blue eyes brightening as he looked once more at the lazy village. "We've got them this time!"

He lifted his hat, waving at his troops, and started his horse back down the slope. As he and Martin neared the base of the hill he shouted: "Boys, we've got them! We'll finish them up and go home to Fort Lincoln."

Adjutant Cooke trooted up to meet them. "Are we going in now, sir?"

"Straight down this valley," Custer told him. "In about a mile, a ravine turns toward the river. When Reno brings them to battle, we'll cross and strike them in the rear."

For five or ten minutes they rode on in gallops and trots, screened by the hills on their left. Just ahead now was the small ravine, and Custer raised his hand, bringing the column to a halt. He wheeled his horse, facing Martin. "Orderly, I want you to take a message to Captain Benteen. Ride as fast as you can and tell him to hurry. Tell him it's a big village and I want him to be quick, and to bring the ammunition packs."

Martin was astonished at how fast Custer rattled off the order, and he wasn't certain he could remember every word of the instructions. Automatically he said, "Yes, sir," and saluted, but at the same time he glanced in perplexity at Adjutant Cooke, whose eyes also revealed surprise.

Cooke signaled Martin to hold steady. "Wait, I'll write out the message." The adjutant fumbled a notebook from his shirt pocket, scribbled hastily, tore out the leaf and gave it to Martin. "Now, Orderly," he said slowly, "ride as fast as you can to Captain Benteen. Take the same trail we came down. If you have time and there's no danger, come back. Otherwise stay with your troop."

Martin saluted, thrust the message inside his shirt, and turned his horse about. He heard Cooke's deep voice: "Is the village so large we'll need more ammunition, sir?"

Before Custer could reply, Martin was trotting back down the column. He held that pace until he passed the rear guard, then urged his mount to a gallop. The weary animal tried desperately, but could not keep to a running speed. For a minute or so Martin slowed to a walk. Glancing back, he saw that the column had turned toward the river.

To maintain a column of four's, Custer was marching on the far slope of the narrow ravine. From Martin's position, the riders appeared to be leaning in their saddles. Hot sunlight glinted off metal equipments, its brilliance sharply defining the different colors of the troop mounts. The sorrels of C Troop were in the lead, followed by the bays of F Troop. In the center were the E Troop grays, appearing almost white against the brownish green of the hills.

Martin looked ahead and saw Mark Kellogg coming along on his mule. The newspaperman kicked impatiently at the animal's flanks. "Custer didn't send you back for me, did he?"

"No, sir, I'm taking a message to Captain Benteen." The trumpeter slowed, but did not stop.

From somewhere beyond the hills, gunfire rattled faintly. "I believe Reno has engaged them!" Kellogg cried. "If this mule doesn't move faster, I'll miss the whole show."

With a wave of his hand, Martin swept on past. The distant firing was more persistent now, and he decided to detour along the ridge. From the elevation where he had gone with Custer, he thought he might be able to sight Benteen's battalion.

He spoke softly to his horse, then dismounted and led the animal along until he could look down into the valley. Instead of the peaceful village he had seen a few minutes before, everything was in turmoil. Reno's men were dismounted and skirmishing down the valley. Hundreds of

Indians, mounted and on foot, were circling and shooting at the soldiers. Beyond the tepees a trail of dust marked the flight of women and children. Far off to the southwest was a thinner dust cloud, probably Benteen's.

Martin remounted and hurried back toward the trail. Halfway down the slope he heard the zing of a bullet, the sudden echo slap of rifle fire. Spurring his horse, he clung close to his saddle. In a gully to the rear, some Indians were waving buffalo robes and firing. Their bullets came close, and once his horse sagged as if hit. Martin grabbed his carbine and prepared to dismount, but the animal regained its footing and sped on down the valley, out of range.

A minute or so later he saw a lone horseman approaching at a steady lope. The rider was not wearing a blue uniform, and Martin halted, watching suspiciously until he was sure the man was not an Indian. As he came nearer Martin recognized him as the general's brother, Boston Custer, civilian forage master with the pack train.

Boston Custer was younger but heavier than either of his brothers. His black hat and long sideburns were covered with dust. "Where's the general?" he shouted, pulling his horse up beside Martin's.

"Right behind the next ridge, you'll find him," Martin replied, and added, "some Indians almost ambushed me back there."

"I'll watch out for them." His pale blue eyes studied the trumpeter. "You are message-bearer?"

"Yes, sir. From the general to Captain Benteen."

"Benteen's back there." He swung his arm vaguely. "He outran the pack train." He lowered his reins, and dashed on down the trail.

Martin watched him for a moment, then tried to increase the speed of his own mount. But the horse seemed completely exhausted and would go no faster than a trot. The sun burned hot. Puffy clouds were drifting in the blue sky. A fine Sunday, too pretty for fighting, Martin thought.

In the same stream where Custer's battalion had watered horses, Martin let his weary animal stand and drink for a minute. Then he went on again at a jog trot. He kept searching the horizon for some sign of Benteen.

Hoofbeats sounded behind him. He swung around, slashed with his quirt, begged the animal to run faster. The horse did its best, but slowed dangerously as the trail steepened.

When Martin shot over the rise, he gasped a prayer of relief. A few hundred yards away was Benteen's battalion, the captain riding in front.

Martin called out, waved his hat, and spurred his horse once more. Glancing over his shoulder, he saw his pursuers swerving back the way they had come.

Benteen had turned the column and was approaching at a fast trot. A few yards behind him was Captain Tom Weir at the head of D Troop. They were kicking up a lot of dust now. Martin let his weary horse slow to a walk. Benteen's hat was flung back and his face looked red as fire under his white mop of hair. "Garibaldi!" he shouted. "You come from Custer?"

"Yes, sir," Martin saluted and handed the written message to the captain. Benteen held it in the sunlight, frowning as he read aloud: " 'Come on. Big village. Be quick. Bring packs.' "

Benteen glanced at the south horizon where the pack train was scattered more than a mile in the rear. Some mules were walking, others trotting, a few running. "Where's the general now?" he asked.

"Down this trail, sir. By now he may have charged the Indian village."

Captain Weir reined up, and Benteen handed him the message.

Martin started to add that Major Reno was already fighting the Indians down river, but Benteen cut him off. "What's the matter with your horse?"

"He's just tired out, I guess, sir."

"Tired out? Look at his hip."

Martin was startled by the amount of blood which had flowed from a bullet wound across his horse's flank.

"You're lucky it was the horse and not you," Benteen said, and turned to Weir. "What do you make of that message, Tom?"

Weir shook his head. "The general can't mean for us to go back for the packs."

"No, and if he's attacking, he'll have no time to wait for them." Benteen pulled his hat brim down. "Garibaldi, go and exchange your mount for one of Captain Weir's spare horses and come back forward."

Martin saluted and started down the cavalry line. Benteen called: "Column half right. March!"

As soon as Martin transferred his saddle to one of the led horses, he galloped back to the head of the column. Benteen was following Custer's trail in a steady trot, but above the beating of hoofs came sounds of firing. In a minute or so they were nearing the base of the hill which Martin had climbed twice that afternoon. The rattle of carbine and rifle fire grew in intensity and seemed to be coming toward them.

"Left—front into line!" They charged up the slope, pistols drawn, and Martin was sure that when they reached the top they would meet a wave of hostile Indians fleeing from Custer's attack. Instead, as he rode out into full view of the Little Big Horn he saw small parties of soldiers climbing a bluff to the right. Other soldiers were in retreat at the riverbank, and the valley across the stream was swarming with Indians.

He heard Benteen's voice: "Ho-o-halt! What the deuce!"

"Must be a thousand red devils down there," Weir cried.

Along the ridge to their right, a horseman was galloping toward them. He wore no hat; a handkerchief fluttered around his forehead. He held up a hand, shouting, and then Martin recognized him as Major Reno. "For God's sake,

Benteen," Reno shouted, "halt your command and help me! I've lost half my men."

"Where's Custer?" Benteen cried.

"I don't know. He went off downstream and I haven't seen or heard anything from him since." Reno halted in front of Benteen.

"I just received a message from him," Benteen said calmly, and read from the scrap of paper: " 'Come on. Big village. Be quick. Bring packs.' Custer must be at the other end of that village down there."

"I don't know," Reno repeated hoarsely, "where he is. He ordered me across the river to charge the Indians. He said he would support me with the whole outfit."

Benteen glanced along the ridge, then back into the valley filling with hostiles. "All right, Major, we'll form a line along that bluff over there and wait for Custer to charge them." He barked commands to his three companies, and they swung to the right. Reno hurried back to reorganize his scattered battalion.

A few minutes later Benteen's men were dismounted, their horses added to those picketed in a square around Surgeon Porter's improvised field hospital. "Come along with me, Garibaldi," Benteen said to Martin. "I'll need an orderly."

The trumpeter was grateful for the privilege of remaining with his white-haired commander. Benteen had filled a pipe and was smoking it calmly, while other officers rushed about shouting wild commands. Major Reno rode back and forth along the ridge, firing his pistol uselessly at the Indians far below.

On the right flank, Indians were keeping up a constant barrage, occasionally charging the slope. "Captain Weir," Benteen ordered, "form your men as skirmishers and drive those rascals away." He turned then to Lieutenant Godfrey and ordered him to form another skirmish line along the bluff.

Still puffing his pipe, Benteen strolled over to Reno's adjutant, Lieutenant George Wallace. "Wallace, put the right of your troop here."

"I have no troop, Captain, only three men."

"Well, stay here with your three men, and don't let them get away. I'll have you looked out for." He turned to Martin. "Garibaldi, go find Lieutenant Godfrey and tell him to extend his line over to this point and start digging in for a siege."

"Yes, sir." Martin started off in a jogging run. Along the ridge, men were beginning to form in a defensive arc. A few were already digging entrenchments, using hatchets, knives, spoons—any piece of metal they could find. Indians were still massed along the river, and many were crossing into a strip of woods at the far right, well out of carbine range.

He saw Godfrey standing with Weir. The tall, restless Godfrey held a hand cupped behind one ear, listening, and was peering northward down the valley.

"It's firing, I tell you Godfrey," Weir was saying. "Heavy firing. But there's too much smoke and dust—I can't make out anything but horses, a pony herd maybe, milling about."

"What's the matter with Custer?" Godfrey demanded impatiently. "Why doesn't he send us word what to do?"

Weir shook his head. "He sent Benteen a message to come and bring the pack mules. What are we staying here for? If Custer's fighting them, we should be on the fly over there."

Martin called Godfrey's name, saluted, and repeated Benteen's order to change position and start his men to digging in.

"Then Benteen means to stay here," Weir cried angrily. "Look, here comes Major Reno. He's the ranking officer. Major Reno!"

Reno pulled his tired horse to a halt. "Yes, Captain?"

Weir motioned down the valley. "Lieutenant Godfrey and I both hear firing over there, sir. We're certain it's Custer."

Martin lingered a moment, then started back to report to

Captain Benteen. Behind him he could hear Weir and Reno shouting excitedly at each other.

Suddenly everything seemed oddly quiet and Martin realized that firing had ceased on the ridge and along the river. The Indians were milling again, some of the warriors on horses were beginning to gallop back toward their village.

"Captain Weir!" The voice was Major Reno's, very angry. Martin stopped and looked back. Almost at the same instant the muffled echoes of volleys fired from far away seemed to float along on the warm summer air.

Weir's booted legs were carrying him rapidly toward the picketed herd. Martin saw him jump on his horse and start off at a gallop northward along the ridge. Weir's men of D Troop were also mounting up and forming file behind him.

Puzzled, Martin turned and saw Benteen striding forward, his pipe held out in one hand. "Godfrey, what in thunder does Weir think he's doing?"

"Going to join Custer, I suppose, sir," Godfrey replied flatly. He pointed below. "And it appears the hostiles down there are doing the same."

Martin's eyes followed the directing line of Lieutenant Godfrey's finger. All the mounted Sioux were wheeling away from the river, leaving only a rear guard of dismounted warriors. Slanting sunlight turned their dust trail to gold. The last warrior in the line was riding a bobtail horse.

15

Bobtail Horse

June 25, afternoon

After returning from a long scout, Bobtail Horse had rested two days in the Cheyenne camp on the Little Big Horn. On the third day he was fidgety for want of something to do, and when Roan Bear came by and said, "Let us go hunt for buffalo," Bobtail Horse replied, "Yes, a hunt will be good. But let us not go far. Long Hair Custer is sure to come here in a day or so, and we must be ready for the fighting."

The two Cheyennes rode out on the prairie for a way and then started north along the Little Big Horn valley, looking for signs of a herd. They saw some antelope grazing near a creek and decided to kill one and take the meat back to camp. After they finished butchering, they were both very hot.

They fastened their ponies to a willow tree and swam in the creek, drinking some of the cold, sweet water. When they came out, Roan Bear picketed his pony so it could graze, and sat in the sun to dry himself.

"Do not let your pony fill himself with grass," Bobtail Horse said.

"But he is hungry," Roan Bear replied.

"If a pony's stomach is too full, he can not run a long way," Bobtail Horse declared. "We must always be ready for the soldiers."

"I am not afraid of the bluecoats," Roan Bear said proudly. "We whipped the soldiers of Three Stars Crook and chased them back toward the Big Horns."

"That is so. I wish I had been there." Bobtail Horse plucked a grass shoot from the earth and nibbled its tender root stem.

Roan Bear talked for awhile about the battle on the Rosebud. Crook's soldiers, he said, had acted very foolishly. They had dismounted and left their horses too far behind, and the Cheyennes and Sioux had cut them off and captured many fine animals.

Bobtail Horse nodded. "It was a great victory. The chiefs have said so. But we have heard Sitting Bull tell of his vision, of many soldiers falling into camp. I have seen them coming from where the sun rises, and they are very fierce. Long Hair Custer has strong medicine."

Roan Bear dried his feet with grass and slipped on his moccasins. "I have told you of the fighting," he said. "Now you must tell me of your scouting. In the Cheyenne council lodge, Two Moons has been full of praise for the bravery of Bobtail Horse."

"I went far into the badlands across the Powder, looking for soldiers," Bobtail Horse said. "One day they came from the direction of the sun's rising—Long Hair Custer with many pony soldiers and some walking soldiers, and big guns drawn by horses, and more wagons than a man can see all at one time. I did as the chiefs told me. I counted the men and horses and wagons and guns. I did not try to take any scalps, because I did not want them to know I was watching. One day I could have killed two of them easily—a scout they call Charley Reynolds and a strange man who does not wear soldier clothes. He carries a little stick with which he makes marks in a little book. They call him Mark Kellogg.

Another time Long Hair Custer and some soldiers came very close to me, but only once did they see me. Charley Reynolds and the Rees chased me, but could not catch me."

Roan Bear yawned and stretched himself. "I think I will sleep for awhile," he said.

"No." Bobtail Horse stood up. "Let us take the meat back to camp. We can sleep in our tepees where it is cooler."

They were about halfway back to camp when they heard sounds of guns. At first there were only a few shots, but there was much dust in the sky to the south, and the firing grew heavier.

"The soldiers have come!" Bobtail Horse cried. "Let us hurry." With his quirt, he slapped his pony into a fast gallop. He was filled with excitement and eagerness for battle.

Very soon they could see the Cheyenne village. Women and children were hurrying toward them, some on horses, most of them on foot. The first people they met were an old woman and an old man. "Long Hair Custer is coming!" the old man cried.

Roan Bear and Bobtail Horse slowed their ponies. "We will give him a good whipping," Roan Bear boasted.

"Where are the Cheyenne warriors?" Bobtail Horse asked. He could see none anywhere.

"Two Moons and the warriors have all gone to fight soldiers in the Hunkpapa village." The old man pointed upstream. "We have sent boys to warn them that Long Hair Custer is coming now to the Cheyenne village!"

Bobtail Horse peered at the tree-fringed river, listening. He could see no movement beyond, and could hear only the babble of women and children, who were running like ants toward them from the village.

"The soldiers come slowly," the old man explained. "They are in a ravine across the river."

Bobtail Horse slapped his quirt down and started forward again with Roan Bear. Squaws were shouting encouragement to them as they went along. He saw two other Cheyennes riding in from the prairie, and signaled them to come quickly.

In a minute the four were riding through the deserted Cheyenne village. Only a few dogs ran about, barking. As soon as they reached the sandy approach to a ford, they could see soldiers across the river—fifty or more soldiers in dark-blue shirts and light-blue trousers with yellow stripes. These soldiers were all riding gray horses in a column of two's. Riding parallel with the gray horse troop, but farther up the slope of the ravine, was a column of sorrels and a column of bays, all moving slowly toward the ford.

Bobtail Horse and his three companions held their ponies steady, watching the soldiers. "We must not let them across the river," Bobtail Horse said. "They will destroy our village."

Roan Bear looked at him. "We are four against two hundred."

Two more Cheyenne warriors were coming along the bank, their ponies lunging in deep sand. "Here are White Shield and Mad Wolf," Bobtail Horse replied. "They are Dog Soldiers and very brave. They will help us fight Long Hair Custer until Two Moons brings the warriors from the Hunkpapa camp."

White Shield held his rifle balanced in one hand, and shook it fiercely at the bluecoats.

Mad Wolf was counting them by opening and closing his fingers. "No one must charge the soldiers now," he warned. "They are too many."

Bobtail Horse did not answer him. "Brave warriors, follow me!" he cried, and all six splashed across the shallow ford.

The soldiers paid no attention to the six Indians, but came on slowly, letting their horses pick their way over rough ground. They seemed very close, with bright sunshine lighting their bearded faces. Their soldier-chief gave a command, and carbines glinted in the sun. The column kept coming.

On his right, Bobtail Horse saw a low ridge. He turned and led his five companions behind it. They dismounted, looped their ponies' reins to tree limbs, and lay down behind the ridge, with rifles pointed at the soldiers.

"When the first horse comes to the sandy place, I will shoot its rider," Bobtail Horse said. "Each of you pick a different soldier and shoot when I do."

But a moment later the soldier-chief halted his men and sent four soldiers forward to scout the ford. Bobtail Horse decided to wait no longer. He fired at the nearest soldier and knocked him from the saddle. The other warriors also fired, but the soldiers went zigzagging on their gray horses back up the hill, and none was hit.

On the slope, a bugle blared. "Now they will charge us," said Mad Wolf.

"No, they are dismounting!" Bobtail Horse cried.

Horse holders were collecting the gray horses and leading them back out of range. Farther up the ridge, the other two columns had halted and seemed to be waiting to see what the gray horse troop would do.

"Let us fool the soldiers," said Bobtail Horse. "They cannot see us, so we will run back and forth behind this ridge, shooting from different places. Maybe they will think we are many."

For a few minutes, Bobtail Horse's trick kept the soldiers at a distance. The men in blue formed in little groups along the slope. Their soldier-chief sent some of the group running forward, but Bobtail Horse and his five companions fired at them and drove them back, wounding some of them. Before the soldiers could advance again, the Cheyennes changed positions and fired from these other places.

But now the other columns were coming, still mounted, in four long lines. These other soldiers held their carbines at ready, and Bobtail Horse knew these mounted ones were going to charge.

"They are too many!" Mad Wolf cried.

About this time Bobtail Horse heard hoofs beating softly on sand. He turned and looked across the river through the trees and saw Two Moons coming with more than a hundred Cheyenne warriors. *"Hi-yi-yi!"* the Cheyennes were crying. They splashed across the river, shaking their shields. *"Hi-yi-yi!"*

Bugles sounded on the slope, and all the soldiers were dismounting. Before their horse holders could move away, carbines snarled along their line front, and the Cheyennes began firing back.

Now there was another rumble of hoofbeats, more and more of them growing steadily louder. Bobtail Horse was startled to see Gall, the great war chief of the Hunkpapas, come charging across the ford in a shower of spray. Behind him was a swirl of Sioux, a hundred, two hundred, three hundred, more even than that. *"Hoka-hey!" Hoka-hey!"* the Hunkpapas shouted as they galloped across in front of Bobtail Horse, never slacking speed but charging the dismounted soldiers of the gray horse troop, flowing over them in a dark flood.

Bobtail Horse and his friends leaped over the ridge and ran up the hill, but the soldiers were running away, some on foot, some on their horses.

From the side of the slope, Bobtail Horse saw still another line of warriors racing along the flats across the river. "Look!" he cried. "It is Crazy Horse and the Oglalla warriors." Crazy Horse did not cross at the ford, but kept going north, with hundreds of warriors galloping behind him.

"Why do the Oglallas not come and help us?" Roan Bear shouted.

"Crazy Horse knows what he is doing," Bobtail Horse said. "He will catch the running soldiers from the other side."

A bullet whined over Bobtail Horse's head. He dropped flat and quickly reloaded his rifle. Gall and the Hunkpapas were forming a great circle now, to ring the soldiers who were trying to make a stand across another ravine. Two Moons and the Cheyennes were farther to the left, chasing some of the soldiers on sorrel horses, who had been cut off from the others.

Bobtail Horse started to go back for his pony, but all of a sudden he saw a dozen or more of the soldiers' gray horses come charging down from the top of the slope. At first he thought soldiers might be riding on them, holding to saddle pommels and clinging to the animals' sides, trying to escape. But when the horses came closer, with manes and tails flying, eyes rolling in fright, he knew they were stampeding without riders.

Roan Bear dodged to one side to escape being trampled. Another one of the Cheyennes was knocked flying. But Bobtail Horse made a mighty leap, caught a mane, and lifted himself into the soldier saddle.

"Hi-yi-yi!" he shouted, and with the reins forced the gray horse close to another one and captured it also. He let the horses run away their fear, guiding them up the floor of the ravine along which the soldiers had come.

It was there that Bobtail Horse saw again for the last time the man he could have easily killed one day back in the badlands across the Powder—the strange white man who did not wear soldier clothes. Now he was riding a mule, all alone, and he seemed to be lost. He was the one the soldiers had called Mark Kellogg.

16

Mark Kellogg

June 25, 4 P.M.–6 P.M.

For a minute or so after he met Trumpeter John Martin coming back along the trail, Mark Kellogg could see the rear guard of Custer's column swinging left into the ravine ahead. The horses were bays, and he thought he recognized Captain Keogh on Comanche in the lead. "Troop I," he said aloud, and then the last set of four's passed out of sight.

"Come alive, Horace!" he shouted to his mule. "We've no time to lose." He wondered what message Custer could be sending back to Benteen. Then he heard a horse running along the rough slope to his right.

Kellogg had his hunting rifle out of its boot before he recognized the rider. Boston Custer waved his hat and turned into the trail. "Where's the general's battalion, Mr. Kellogg?" he called.

"Just ahead," the newspaperman replied. "Down that ravine to the left." He kicked the mule's ribs, in an effort to keep pace with the horse. "I don't suppose you'd care to swap mounts, would you, Boston?"

Boston Custer laughed and shook his head. "I don't want

to miss the show, Mr. Kellogg. Major Reno's already charging at the south end."

"I've heard the firing. Rather heavy at times."

"Stirred up a lot of Indians. Like hornets. I had to outrun a pack of them. You'd better put a burr under that mule's tail and get out of here." Boston Custer looked anxiously ahead. "I'll be moving on, Mr. Kellogg. Good luck."

"I'll see you at the fighting, Boston."

The horse sped away, and by the time Kellogg reached the turn into the ravine, Boston Custer was far down the narrow passage. The column's rear troop was also still in sight. Beyond lay the timbered valley of the Little Big Horn.

Because Custer's troopers were moving over grass, they left little dust in the air, but the sun was almost directly in Kellogg's eyes. He pulled his hat brim down and pleaded with the stubborn mule, but the animal seemed reluctant to go any farther. In disgust, Kellogg dismounted and walked along in front, tugging at the mule's tie rope.

A patter of rifle fire echoed from the valley. The show, as Boston Custer had described it, was opening. "Blast it!" Kellogg cried. He leaped on the mule, slapped its flank with a rope, and turned toward the top of the ridge. Concealment was no longer necessary, and he hoped he might witness some of the fighting from the high point above.

Before he reached the ridge top, the irregular firing had increased to a steady drumming intermingled with war cries of Indians and soldiers. A few feet from the summit, Kellogg abandoned his mule and ran forward. In a moment the valley lay before him. Nearest the river was E Troop, dismounted, its gray horses formed in a sort of oval in the rear. Tom Custer's C Troop was also dismounted, horse holders scrambling to the rear with its sorrels. F Troop was still mounted on its bays in a line formation, and seemed to be supporting C. Farther north, I and L moved in and out of Kellogg's view, both troops having difficulty keeping formations across ground slashed by gullies.

Just beyond the farthest point of the gray horse troop was a mass of mounted Indians churning across a shallow ford. Kellogg assumed they were being driven from the rear by Reno's attack. In another few minutes, he thought, the fight will be over. And here I am a mile from the action.

He took out his notebook and pencil and made a hasty sketch, studying the terrain between him and the battleground. The quickest way there would be down the floor of the ravine. He glanced at his mule. The animal nibbled daintily at choice sprigs of grass, disdaining any interest in the noisy conflict below.

With a rude comment, Kellogg mounted again, angling down the slope. He had gone about a hundred yards when he saw two gray horses running toward him. An Indian was mounted upon one, holding the other closely alongside. At first, Kellogg supposed the rider might be one of the Crow scouts. He stared at the Indian, and the Indian stared back at him. Then the Indian's rifle barrel twinkled in sunlight.

Kellogg jerked on his rein, knowing he had no time to get his own rifle into position. "Ho!" he yelled, pounding the mule with his rope and looking back over his shoulder. The Indian managed to fire one shot, but was almost unseated when his horse lunged.

"Come on, Horace!" Kellogg cried, and for once the mule responded. Before the Indian could gather his horse and fire again, Kellogg was over the ridge. He grabbed his hunting rifle and turned down into a shallow gully screened by sagebrush. When he faced toward the battlefield, he was startled by what he saw.

Hundreds of Indians were swarming over E Troop's position. Patches of dark blue lay motionless along the slope. The horse herd was gone, at least a dozen of the gray mounts dead or dying. C Troop was scattering in confusion, and F was withdrawing mounted. Indians were still crossing the ford, swarming in all directions, like angered ants. Gun smoke and dust swirled over everything.

Bugles sounded from the north where Troops I and L were formed, with the regimental flag flying as a rallying point. Indians streamed up gullies on both flanks of their position.

Where was Reno? Kellogg glanced hopefully across the muddied ford toward the tepee village, but there was no fighting there, no smoke, no firing. What had gone wrong?

No time for guessing, he thought. I am a newspaperman and I must tell the story of this fight and get it back to Bismarck. He held the mule steady, cradling his rifle, scratching fragments of phrases on a sheet of his notebook.

Whee-e-ean! A bullet knocked earth from the gully wall a few inches from Kellogg's head. He slid out of the saddle, dropping his notebook, raising his rifle. From the direction of fire, he knew his enemy was behind him. He crawled along the gully a few feet, raised up, and searched the ridge. There he was, skulking in the shadow of a brush clump. Kellogg pulled his trigger. The Indian dropped, then darted rapidly away in a running crouch.

They will soon be all around me, he thought. To survive, I must work my way around this ridge and try to join Keogh and Calhoun. Custer must be there with the regimental flag, and Custer's luck surely will save some of us.

Keeping low, he returned to the mule, removed his saddlebag, and then started crawling along the gully. In a minute or so he was in the open, but he sighted another wash farther down. He drew a deep breath, ducked, and ran. The ditch was shallower than he had thought, and he flattened himself, scurrying like a lizard. He raised his head, then stood erect, trying to orient himself on the regimental flag. The flag was in motion. Troops I and L were moving farther back to a higher ridge.

A second later, Kellogg heard the arrows. *Whit, whit, whit.* He saw them streak past. *Whit-tuk! S-thung!* He felt the pain like a red-hot iron bar driving into his back. He stood rooted in his tracks for a moment, reaching desperately for the arrow. His hand came away stained with blood.

Pain burned up into his shoulders and neck, then numbed; he dropped down and began crawling again. He must reach Custer's headquarters position. A surgeon would be there to remove the arrow.

Kellogg crawled until his hands and knees were raw. All his strength seemed to be flowing away, and he lay on his side in the shaded edge of the gully, breathing heavily. Sounds of battle came from all directions—cries and whoops and a screaming of bullets, the rattle and slap of gunfire.

How much of luck there is in life, he thought. A whim of chance had brought him to this field of death. His fingers touched the wide leather belt around his waist, Clem Lounsberry's belt, lucky talisman. But for chance, Lounsberry would be where he was now, and he would be in Bismarck. "My Civil War Belt," Lounsberry had said proudly. "Take it for luck, Mark. It saved my life once. See the old bloodstain on it."

There would be plenty of blood on Lounsberry's belt this time, he thought. Again he tried to reach the arrow. Charley Reynolds had told him about Sioux arrows, how the shafts were grooved so that blood would keep flowing from a wound unless they were removed.

A burst of firing sounded very close, a drumfire of carbines—which meant that soldiers must be near him. He forced himself to his knees, resting his elbows on a shelf of dark-gray earth, looking northward along the hogback ridge. The regimental flag had vanished, but a guidon was fluttering on a distant knoll, too far away for him to distinguish the troop.

A cool wind fanned his fevered face, shaking the sagebrush and greasewood bushes, bending the high grass along the fringes of the ridge. Suddenly the blue and yellow colors of the 7th Regiment's flag rose from the earth not more than a quarter of a mile away. It fluttered higher, and then I Troop was there. A black-tailed, black-maned buckskin pranced along—Comanche with Captain Keogh in the saddle. Keogh's sharp-pointed chin beard was glossy black in the sun. They were coming up from a ravine. The troop was in four's, with a file of scouts on its right flank firing steadily at Indians coming up from the river. In a steady trot, the column moved to the highest point on the hogback and halted.

If I shout they can hear me, Kellogg thought. He tried to cry out, but the sound died in his throat, a gurgling cough. Keogh had turned Comanche about, and was facing his men. At the same moment, Troop L appeared out of the same ravine, Lieutenant Calhoun guiding his men alongside Troop I.

Keogh's gauntleted hand was up. He was shouting orders. The men in both troops lifted their carbines, aiming skyward. To Kellogg's astonishment, they fired four volleys in rapid succession—at no target! The blast roared in his ears. Dense smoke rolled away in the wind. He could see troopers firing now at sniping hostiles who were coming up from the river, darting from sagebrush cover to little gullies, always moving closer.

Kellogg wondered why Keogh had fired the volleys. The sound was surely meant for someone to hear. Reno, of course. And where was Reno?

Painfully, Kellogg turned around, facing south. His vision blurred, and then he thought he could see a tiny spot of moving color on a high point far up the valley. It must be a guidon, one of Reno's guidons. He wondered if Reno was answering Keogh's signal for help. Or was Reno also calling for help?

He leaned forward again on the little shelf of gray sun-baked earth, expecting Keogh to come along the hogback. But the troopers were dismounting, preparing to make a stand against new waves of hostiles surging up from the river.

Suddenly Kellogg caught a flash of movement from the east side of the ridge—another line of hostiles coiling like an endless snake, racing to attack Keogh's rear! Again Kellogg tried to cry out, but he knew that even if he could shout a warning, no one would hear him above the din of battle.

This new swarm of enemies seemed to have sprung from the earth, and they came like the wind, driving their horses up the back slope, shaking bows and rifles and lances. Their war cries broke all at once, an eerie voice sound that chilled the blood.

It is no use any more, Kellogg thought. We are all doomed.

As the attack wave swept across the ridge, Kellogg saw the leader in all his war rigging, whipping his horse with a strip of rawhide fastened around his wrist. He wore red squaw cloth around his waist. His shoulders were naked and painted red. His hair was hanging loose, two feathers fluttering in it. He carried a rifle in a fringed covering across his back, and was firing arrows from a bow. His pony was hung with red tassels, the haunches streaked with red paint in jagged lines like lightning.

This warrior is a chief, Kellogg thought. Charley Reynolds described him to me. This is Crazy Horse.

17

CRAZY HORSE

June 25, 3 P.M.–sundown

Ho-he! It was a great chase after those soldiers who came to kill Sitting Bull's Hunkpapa people.

When Crazy Horse arrived from the Oglalla village with his warriors, Gall had driven the bluecoats into some woods and the fighting was growing fierce. Then all of a sudden the frightened soldier-chief led his men out of the woods in a fast ride for the bluffs across the river. *"Hokay-hey!"* Crazy Horse shouted to his Oglallas, and the chase began. It was like a buffalo hunt all the way to the river. Crazy Horse fired many times with his Winchester, and more than one bluecoat felt the sting of his bullets.

At the river crossing, the warriors rushed the last of the soldiers, knocking some of them into the water with war clubs. When that was finished, Crazy Horse took pity on his yellow pinto. He dismounted to let the tired pony suck wind into its lungs.

Some of the Oglallas started to cross the river after the soldiers, but Crazy Horse called them back. "We have whipped the bluecoats," he said. "After we rest our horses, we will cross the river farther down, where they cannot shoot at us in the water."

After a minute or so he saw Sitting Bull come riding with Gall. Crazy Horse lifted his rifle in greeting. *"Ho-ee!"* he cried. "The Sioux peoples have won a great victory!"

Gall's thick chest heaved under his red shirt. "Sitting Bull has seen more soldiers going down on the other side of the river," he said, in his deep voice. "Two Moons and his Cheyennes are riding back to fight them."

"The Cheyennes are good warriors," Crazy Horse answered quickly. "But their numbers are few in this camp."

"That is so," Gall agreed. "My Hunkpapa ponies have not run so far as those of your Oglallas. I will take my warriors and go help the Cheyennes."

Crazy Horse cased his rifle in the fringed covering which he wore across his back. "The Oglallas will join in this new fight," he said earnestly. "We have fresh ponies in our camp."

Sitting Bull nodded and said: "It is good that our Sioux families are together and strong for the fighting. I will stay here with the warriors who have no horses and keep them shooting at the soldiers on that hill over there. Gall will go first, with his warriors. Crazy Horse, with fresh ponies, can go around and catch those other soldiers between you like rabbits."

"Washte! It is good!" Gall cried. "Let us ride like the wind!" He started his pony off at a gallop, summoning his warriors to follow him.

Crazy Horse blew on his bone whistle and began shouting the news to his assembling Oglallas. Soon their ponies were milling all about. Gall's Hunkpapas moved quickly down the valley, and then Crazy Horse on his pinto led the Oglallas into their settling dust.

Before a man would have time to build a campfire, Crazy Horse was around the river bend and approaching the Oglalla village. He saw no signs of soldiers, but somewhere beyond the timbered river a few scattered shots were being fired.

This firing had alarmed the squaws, and many were flying like birds out upon the prairie, seeking safety. When the squaws saw the warriors coming, those who were riding ponies hurried back to exchange them for the tired ones of their men.

Crazy Horse was pleased to see his wife Black Shawl waiting by their tepee, holding a horse saddled and ready for him. The horse was a sorrel he had captured from Three Stars Crook on the Rosebud. *"Ha-eye-ya!"* he shouted to Black Shawl. "You have dressed my horse with your red tassels and painted him with my red lightning marks. This is a good sign, Black Shawl." He leaped from the yellow pinto and mounted the sorrel. "Take the pinto and go far out," he told her, and then danced the big sorrel around.

Less than a mile downstream, the Hunkpapas were splashing across a ford, their guns beginning to roar, the soldiers' guns chattering in reply. "Warriors, let us ride to another victory!" Crazy Horse shouted. "It is a good day for bluecoats to die!" They swept away, swinging left to avoid the sandy border of the river, and in the time it would take to light a pipe, Crazy Horse was at the ford where Gall's warriors were still crossing. He kept the sorrel galloping straight ahead.

Glancing through an opening in the trees, he saw the slope where Gall was fighting the soldiers. Gray horses were running about, and bluecoats were scattering back up the ridge.

At the south end of the Cheyenne village, the river turned sharply to the east, forming a shallow sand bar. Slowing to a walk, Crazy Horse led the way through some trees, and then he was quickly across the river.

For a moment he held the sorrel steady. On a hill to the right, a bright blue-and-yellow flag fluttered. Bugles sounded there, and some mounted soldiers began moving away along a ridge, taking the flag with them.

"Let us ride around them!" Crazy Horse shouted. "Then they will be caught between Oglallas and Hunkpapas!"

He pounded the sorrel with his quirt, circling the hill until he reached the shady side of the ridge. Upon the narrow hogback, the soldiers marched away from him in a steady trot, their big flag flying at the front. But now the Oglalla ponies could run straight ahead over level ground, and soon they would overtake the soldiers.

Crazy Horse looked back. His warriors were galloping in a single file and by two's and three's—hundreds of them; so many he could not see the last riders. We are like a great arrow pointed at the bluecoat invaders.

For some reason the soldiers were halting. Perhaps they were going to make a stand. But they were not facing toward the Ogallas. They raised their guns and fired all at one time, a mighty blast like thunder. Four times they fired at the sky, and the smoke of powder rolled thick around them.

Crazy Horse wondered why they would waste their bullets so foolishly. Now they were dismounting and shooting down the other side of the ridge. Gall and his Hunkpapas would be there. And now the Oglallas were at the soldiers' backs. It was time to turn the ponies.

No need for a gun, Crazy Horse thought. He raised his bow, pointing toward the ridge top. *"Hoka-hey!"* he shouted, and swerved his horse up the slope. The voices of his warriors echoed the war cry in a wild rush of sound. Startled faces of soldiers turned in their direction, but the Oglallas gave them no time to fire. Crazy Horse whipped an arrow in clean flight from his bow.

The first Oglalla charge broke the soldiers' line. Rifles roared and arrows flew in deathly whispers. Then the fighting was close, with lances and clubs, and carbines used as clubs.

Troopers and horses were cut down, but a brave soldier-chief with a black pointed chin beard rallied his men into a tight circle and they poured a fierce fire into the Oglallas. Crazy Horse pulled his warriors away in a zigzag withdrawal. "Fight together," he told them. "Fight like the bluecoats. Throw your arrows and bullets into them all at one time. Do not try to count *coup.*" Then he led them back up the slope.

In the second charge, ponies and warriors went down under a hail of bullets, but Crazy Horse knew he had victory in his hands. Gall's warriors were coming strong now from the other side of the ridge. Oglallas, Hunkpapas, Minneconjous and Cheyennes galloped in, circled, charged, circled and charged.

The soldier-chief and his men were not afraid to die. With one knee down on the ground, they held their guns steady until the Sioux came very close; then they would fire—all at the same time. They were very brave men.

But they could not withstand attacks coming from both sides of the ridge, and they began retreating along the hogback, toward the other band of soldiers on the hill. A forktailed guidon was flying there. The retreating ring of soldiers grew smaller and smaller. Dead horses and men piled up, hindering the Sioux in their rushes.

Around Crazy Horse, bullets were humming like bees. This was the fiercest battle he could remember. He had never heard such a screaming of horses nor such loud war cries from Indians and soldiers. His arrows were all gone, and he had to take his rifle and add to the roar of the firing.

Suddenly out of the soldier circle a man dashed away on a horse, heading for the hill where the other soldiers were. He was not wearing soldier clothing. His hair was long and yellow but he had no beard. "It is Long Hair Custer!" a warrior shouted, and a dozen others took up the chase. For a minute or so the fighting quieted down. Indians and soldiers were watching the running horses.

"He is not the Long Hair," a young Cheyenne said to Crazy Horse.

"No," said Crazy Horse. "The Long Hair would not run away and leave his men."

"That one is the Long Hair's brother," the Cheyenne said.

The Long Hair's brother had a fast horse with good wind, and soon only three warriors were left in the chase. One of them was wearing a buffalo-horn headdress. The warriors fired but missed. The soldiers cheered. Then the warrior with the buffalo horn fired again and hit the Long Hair's brother. He rode for a few paces more and fell from his saddle.

"Look!" the Cheyenne cried. "Now some of the others are trying to run away!"

It was so. The soldier-chief with the black beard pointed like an arrow was leading the soldiers down a little ravine toward the river. Crazy Horse watched with admiration. This soldier-chief scorned all the bullets and arrows of his enemies. He was riding a fine-spirited buckskin—black-tailed, black-maned, with a white star on its forehead. The soldier-chief kept turning his horse to shield his men. The horse was bleeding from bullet wounds, but was as brave as its rider and did not flinch. Four or five mounted men were riding with their soldier-chief, and at least a dozen soldiers on foot were running close to the horses.

Crazy Horse hurried along the edge of the ravine. "These are brave men," he said to himself. "They will not give up and die." But he knew they could never reach the river alive. More than a hundred warriors were following them, and nothing the soldier-chief could do would stop all the bullets and arrows. Some of the soldiers were badly wounded. One was bleeding from the mouth while he ran.

At last the soldier-chief ordered his men to rush out of the ravine and form a circle with their horses on the slope. The soldiers slew their horses and lay down behind them, and kept shooting at the warriors. The soldier-chief did not kill his buckskin, but commanded it to lie down, and he lay there shooting at the warriors until they swarmed over the circle and killed him and all his soldiers.

"Truly these are the bravest men the Sioux peoples have ever fought," Crazy Horse said.

Now there were no soldiers anywhere along the ridge. Those who had survived were gathered on the hill over to the north, where their fork-tailed flag was still flying.

Crazy Horse pointed his rifle toward the hilltop. "Let us go and finish it!" he cried, and the Oglallas went galloping, hundreds and hundreds of them in a haze of smoke and dust.

The big sorrel was tired from all the running and circling, and Crazy Horse let him go in an easy canter. Warriors were swarming all over the hill, and more were coming from the river and along the ridge.

On the crest of the hill, the last of the soldiers were in two rings around their flag, firing volleys. Crazy Horse saw no reason to hurry. The soldiers' ammunition would not last for long.

Some young Cheyennes, eager to count *coups,* made a dash right up to the first ring of soldiers, and two or three went down with their ponies. The others rushed in and struck the soldiers with clubs and *coup* sticks.

Crazy Horse urged his sorrel to a faster pace, shouting warnings to the younger Oglallas who were charging in too close. "We have won a victory this day!" he cried. "And good warriors have died. Let us not throw our lives away for nothing."

The soldiers were killing most of the reckless Cheyennes. A tall soldier was wrestling with one of them. He wrenched the Cheyenne's rifle away, while the Cheyenne fought back with his quirt. The soldier hit the Cheyenne with his fists, grabbed his hair braids, and shook him to the ground. Another soldier shot the Cheyenne with a pistol.

"Counting *coup* is no way to win battles," Crazy Horse growled. "Let us worry the soldiers by running and circling until they shoot away all their bullets. Then we will rush them."

But the warriors would not wait that day on the Little Big Horn. They came from every direction, the Cheyennes and all the peoples of the Sioux-Hunkpapas, Minneconjous, Sans Arcs, Brules and Oglalles—sweeping up the hill like a wind-driven prairie fire. Crazy Horse was carried along with them.

A few minutes before the end he saw the Long Hair inside the last ring of soldiers with dead horses heaped all around them. The great soldier-chief's hair was cut short, but it was the color of grass when frost comes. His face showed no fear. He stood like a sheaf of corn with all the ears fallen around him.

In one of the last charges, Crazy Horse rode right up to the red-and-white guidon. The banner hung at an angle, a dying soldier propped against the staff. Crazy Horse seized the flag and waved it high in the air.

By this time very few bullets were coming from the soldiers. The warriors could have finished them off with clubs, but they hung back for a minute or so, as if they did not want to end the fighting.

At the end there was only the Long Hair and one soldier kneeling. Suddenly the Long Hair's booted legs sagged beneath him. As he fell he fired point-blank with a pistol, killing a charging Hunkpapa warrior. The Long Hair lifted his head, laughing. It was a taunting laugh. He rose up on his hands and tried another shot, but his pistol would not fire. Then the warriors charged, and that was the end of the fighting on the hill.

Crazy Horse rode in among the warriors, crying: "Do not scalp the Long Hair! He was a great chief!" Some of the Sioux struck the dead soldier-chief with their *coup* sticks, but that was all. The Long Hair was too brave for scalping.

Gall rode up, his broad face shining with triumph. The war chief's red shirt was ripped across his barrel chest. Along one shoulder a flesh wound was marked in dried blood. With his open hand, he made a sweeping gesture at the battlefield. "These men who came with the Long Hair," he said, "were as good men as ever fought."

Crazy Horse nodded. "It was hard fighting," he said, and raised the captured guidon so that the wind whipped it straight out from its staff. "I have been in many hard fights but I never saw such brave men."

An Oglalla boy came riding on a colt. He stopped to admire the guidon flying above Crazy Horse. "It is yours," Crazy Horse said, passing the staff into the boy's hands. "Remember it was taken from brave men by the brave men of your people."

The boy's eyes sparkled with pleasure. He thanked Crazy Horse and rode away on his colt, wagging the red-and-white flag from side to side.

Although there was no more firing, the battlefield was still noisy with calls and shouts and the keening of squaws who were taking away their dead. Some warriors were helping wounded comrades back toward the tepee villages. Others were taking booty from slain soldiers. They took saddles and guns and tobacco. They chased the few horses not yet claimed. They took blankets, knives, bugles, boots and uniforms. From all the camps, squaws and children came running along the slope and ridge top, collecting spent arrows and searching for prizes overlooked by the warriors.

Shots sounded suddenly from a nearby ravine. Gall's head raised alertly. "Our warriors have found a skulking soldier," he said. "I told them to run through every sage patch and gully to see that none escapes."

Crazy Horse and Gall let their mounts take them slowly back along the ridge where the fighting had been the fiercest. Two Cheyenne women were stripping dead soldiers, collecting shiny pieces of metal which the white men called money.

They found pieces of green paper with the metal. The squaws considered the green paper worthless for ornament, and gave it to their children.

One of Gall's warriors, Little Soldier, came up from a ravine with six cartridge belts slung over one shoulder. *"Hohe!"* Little Soldier cried. "It was a great fight, but the soldiers killed my pony, and now I must walk."

"If those cartridge belts are filled," said Gall, "you can trade them for a pony."

"There is not one cartridge," replied Little Soldier. "The bluecoats fought very hard."

"Look along there," Crazy Horse told him, pointing. "A horse is standing by some dead soldiers."

"Hop-o!" Little Soldier shaded his eyes against the setting sun. "I will take that horse even though it is wounded." He went running toward the horse, which was a fine buckskin with black tail and mane and a white star on its forehead.

"That is the horse of a brave soldier-chief," Crazy Horse said to Gall. "The one who wore the arrow-pointed beard on his chin."

They turned their mounts and came to the ring of dead horses and men. All the soldiers had been scalped except their chief, who lay on his back. His shirt had been stripped off, but no one had touched the medal which hung around his neck by a silken cord.

Little Soldier was staring at the medal. "It is strong medicine," he said. "A picture of a young sheep carrying a flag on a cross piece."

Crazy Horse noticed that the hand of the dead soldier-chief still gripped the reins of his horse, which stood quietly with head down. Blood trickled from the animal's neck. "The Great Spirit saved this horse," he said softly.

"It is so," Little Soldier declared. "I have no horse, but I cannot take a horse when a dead man is holding the reins."

"Perhaps it will die soon anyway," Gall said. "It has many wounds." He swung his moccasins out from the stirrups, stretching his stout legs. "Let us go now and tell Sitting Bull of our great victory. Then we will finish those other soldiers on the bluff by the river." He led off in a trot.

In a minute or so they turned down a sandy ravine slanting toward the river. Gall's pony shied suddenly. A white man, not wearing soldier clothes, lay slumped over the edge of the ditch. He had an arrow in his back, and was dead.

Farther along was a saddlebag and some scattered papers and other objects. Crazy Horse swung down and picked up a razor and a mirror. "I will take these to Black Shawl," he said. Gall was looking back impatiently. Then Crazy Horse noticed a curled scrap of deerskin. He flattened it against the packed sand.

"A curious thing!" he cried. "Here is one of Sitting Bull's picture writings!"

Gall wheeled his pony. His heavy-lidded eyes blinked at the drawing. It was Sitting Bull on a horse, shooting an arrow into a soldier. He grunted deep in his throat. "We will take it to Sitting Bull. Perhaps he will understand how it came here."

"It is some kind of magic," Crazy Horse said wonderingly.

They rode on to the ford which had been churned into a mire by thousands of hoofs. Some Cheyenne children were already playing along the bank, as if there had never been any battle.

Crazy Horse leaned from his saddle to examine the images a little girl was fashioning from damp clay. She smiled up at him, holding a tiny mud horse in her grimy hands. To make a saddle, she had folded one of the green pieces of paper found with the metal money of the dead soldiers. Crazy Horse handed her a red feather, and went on to overtake the impatient Gall.

As soon as they passed through the Hunkpapa village, they saw Sitting Bull riding down from a hill across the river. They turned and splashed through the water to meet him. The great chief's face was solemn, but his eyes shone like stars. His single eagle feather was bobbing as he rocked in his saddle.

"We have killed them all!" Gall cried.

Sitting Bull halted his horse and made an expressive gesture, holding his hands out palms up. "Many soldiers fell into camp this day," he replied. "We have shown the White Father that we cannot be driven upon reservations."

Gall grunted and said: "We will go now and finish the ones on that bluff over there."

Sitting Bull shook his head. "More soldiers have come there with mules carrying much ammunition. They have dug themselves into holes like prairie dogs. If we try to kill them now, they will kill ten times as many of us."

"We do not need more killing this day," Crazy Horse agreed.

"But we cannot let them go away unpunished," Gall protested.

Sitting Bull shrugged. "They cannot get away, and no more soldiers can come to them. The Sioux peoples are all around them."

"I will go and look into this," Gall said.

"Shoot at them occasionally, but do not charge them," Sitting Bull warned. "There is no water on that hill. They will fall into our hands when thirst burns in their throats and makes them mad for drink."

Gall made a sign that he understood and rode away. He was a war chief and it was his duty to be where his warriors were.

Crazy Horse handed Sitting Bull the deerskin pictograph. "I found this on the battlefield," he said, "near a dead white man who did not wear soldier clothes."

As he stared at the painted skin Sitting Bull made a hissing noise between his teeth. "Truly there is strong magic here today!" he cried.

"I saw it was the picture writing of Sitting Bull," Crazy Horse added softly.

"It has something to do with my great vision," the chief declared. "This drawing went away from me at the time the vision came in the Sun Dance lodge. And now the Sun has shown it to me again."

"It is strong medicine," Crazy Horse said.

They turned and rode back across the river, Crazy Horse halting briefly to scoop up water in one hand to wash the dust from his throat. When they came to the trail, Sitting Bull turned toward the Hunkpapa village. "I go to my tepee to give thanks to the Great Spirit," he said.

Crazy Horse sighed with weariness. "And I shall lie and rest in the shade by the woods there. Suddenly all my strength has gone away from me."

"After a hard fight, it is like that," Sitting Bull told him. "But tonight there will be dancing and great celebrations around all our campfires."

Crazy Horse rode to the edge of the thick woods where the first soldiers had taken cover before they ran away to the bluffs. A small stream trickled there, and he picketed his sorrel so that it could drink. Then he lay down on a grassy place and closed his eyes. The sun was gone and the day was fast going away.

From the woods came distant sounds—trampled leaves and brush, an occasional voice cry, the *bang-bang* of a gun. More distant rifle fire sounded from the bluffs.

Suddenly he heard voices very near at hand, and when he opened his eyes he grabbed up his rifle. Right in front of him were five or six bluecoats. The wearers of the uniforms laughed at him. They were young Hunkpapa braves dressed in clothing taken from the Long Hair's men. One of them was Little Soldier.

"It is said there are still some bluecoats hiding in these woods," Little Soldier explained. "We will fool them with their own clothing and then kill them."

Crazy Horse put his rifle down. "Take care that you do not fool your own people," he growled, "and be killed by them."

The young braves moved silently into the woods, and he relaxed and closed his eyes again. For a minute or so as dusk came on, everything was quiet and peaceful along the river. The country here is good, he thought. There is rich grass for the ponies and sweet water. The prairie sparkles with flowers of yellow and red and blue. Buffaloes are plentiful in the valleys. The Sioux peoples belong here, and no man has a right to put out his hand and tell us that we should not go where we please. But killing is always a bad thing, and the White Father's arm is long and will surely be raised in anger against his red children. Yet, it is possible the White Father's soldiers have learned their lesson, and there will be peace.

His ears, always alert, caught the sound of moving brush, like a whisper far down in the woods. Little Soldier and the young braves perhaps. But then he heard a white man's voice faintly calling: "O'Neill! Trooper O'Neill!"

18

Trooper Thomas O'Neill

June 25–26

When Lieutenant De Rudio went across the dry creek to recover the A Troop guidon and was rushed by Indians, Big Fritz Sivertsen yelled: "Scatter, boys! Head for the river!" Tom O'Neill ducked his head and plunged into the brush. For a minute or so he followed Sivertsen, but soon fell behind. Then Big Fritz vanished in some trees. O'Neill desperately hurried after him, but his foot caught in a tangle of vines and he fell suddenly, his nose striking a tree root.

He lay half stunned, with blood gushing from his nose. His throat filled with it, choking him. He coughed and sat up, shaking his head. He listened, trying to locate Sivertsen and the others, but he could hear only the shrill whistles of Indians searching for them.

After awhile he decided to go back and try to find Lieutenant De Rudio. He heard low voices coming from the dry wash, and when he peered through the brush he was surprised to see De Rudio with two men who were leading horses. One was a half-breed scout, Billy Jackson. The other was Fred Girard, an interpreter who had been riding with the scouts.

"Our only chance," De Rudio was saying, "is to conceal ourselves until nightfall."

"How in thunder can we hide these horses with the woods full of prowling hostiles?" Girard asked. The interpreter's grizzly beard wagged under a crumpled wide-brimmed hat. He seemed angry at everything and everybody.

"I know a place they'll be safe," De Rudio assured him, and started up the dry creek bed.

O'Neill stepped through the bushes, and Billy Jackson's rifle covered him instantly. O'Neill whispered hoarsely: "Lieutenant!"

"Where'd he come from?" Girard asked in surprise.

O'Neill stumbled down the bank into the sand. De Rudio caught his arm, steadying him. "You been war clubbed, O'Neill?"

"No, sir." O'Neill wiped a fresh flow of blood from his nose with his handkerchief. "Tripped and fell. I think the others made it to the river."

"Come on." De Rudio started off again, impatiently. Around a bend in the wash, was a thick stand of green ash, vines and underbrush. "Picket your horses in there, Girard." Girard and the half-breed led their mounts into this shaded copse while De Rudio and O'Neill kept an alert watch. From the sounds in the woods, O'Neill guessed that most of the Sioux were moving away from them toward the river.

"It'll do," Girard said. "Now what about us?"

"Over here," De Rudio told him. "I hid in this place a few minutes ago with a hundred Indians passing in pistol shot." He turned up a grassy ditch for a few yards, pushed through a thorny patch of brush, and dropped down into a hole. The others followed him in. It was large enough for the four of them to lie comfortably, and was surrounded by bushes which curved inward, making it appear to be a solid clump.

"If they find us here," Girard said, "we haven't got a chance."

"Keep your voice down," De Rudio whispered. "We have to die sometime, Girard, and we'll die like brave men. But I intend to get out of this scrape."

The afternoon dragged away. None of them had any food or water, and their tongues felt thick in their mouths. O'Neill's nose bled at times, and he had to fight to keep from coughing. Late in the day, several squaws passed along the creek bed within a few yards of them. They were carrying clothing and other objects taken from the soldiers.

Terrific firing was going on up and down the river, and each of them made wild guesses as to what was happening to their comrades.

At last twilight came, slowly at first, and then the woods were dark. Campfires glimmered beyond the trees, and they could hear the Indians beginning their victory dances.

"Let's get the horses, Girard," De Rudio whispered.

They left the hole and started toward the copse, walking slowly, saying nothing. It was so dark in the wash that O'Neill took a wrong turn, and soon he could see no one, or hear no one. "O'Neill!" De Rudio called hoarsely, "Trooper O'Neill!"

"Here," he answered gratefully, and then felt someone seize him from behind and Billy Jackson's voice was whispering: "Be quiet!"

"What did you find, Billy?" De Rudio asked softly.

The scout released O'Neill. "Some young Sioux braves in our uniforms, heading for the river. I heard them say Crazy Horse was resting nearby."

"Crazy Horse! Then we'd better hurry." The shapes of two horses loomed up, and De Rudio whispered to Girard: "I'll take hold of your horse's tail, Girard. O'Neill will hold on to the tail of Billy Jackson's horse. If we get separated, we'll never find each other in this blackness. Move out. Crazy Horse may have heard us."

When they came out of the woods, dim moonlight and bright campfires along the valley gave enough light so that O'Neill and De Rudio could walk beside the horses. They had gone about a mile when they saw eight or ten mounted Indians coming toward them. Girard and Jackson angled their horses away from them, De Rudio and O'Neill keeping close to the sides of the animals. The Indians passed without challenging, evidently taking them for tribesmen.

Opposite the bluffs where Major Reno's men had sought safety, several large fires were blazing. O'Neill could see silhouetted Indians jumping and dancing. Some were shaking rattles, blowing whistles, beating drums, whooping and yelling. Others formed in dance circles, their combined voices floating across the semidarkness: *"Huh-ha, huh-ha, eh-hah, eh-hah, eh-hah."*

Girard and Jackson halted. "This is close as I want to be to those scalp dancers, Lieutenant," the interpreter whispered.

"All right, turn to the riverbank."

Across the Little Big Horn, the bluffs towered dark against a hazy moonlit sky. The river purled at their feet, black as ink. A splash startled them, and then they saw the trail of a beaver swimming in the water.

"O'Neill," De Rudio whispered. "Lower yourself in the river and see how deep it is." Holding to a bush with one hand, O'Neill dropped into the water. An icy shock swept from his toes to his neck, the swift current almost jerking him away. De Rudio helped him out.

"Too swift, sir."

"Let me try. Hold my wrist." The lieutenant plunged in and came out gasping in Italian. "Ice water," he said. "You're right, O'Neill. Likely drown us and the horses."

O'Neill dipped his cavalry hat in the stream and offered water to the lieutenant. "At least it's good to drink, sir."

De Rudio took several long swallows. "I'd forgotten how good water can be," he said. "Sweetest I ever tasted."

O'Neill had passed the hat to Girard and Jackson. After they had all slaked their thirsts, they continued upstream, searching for a ford.

Noticing a wide place in the river, O'Neill waded out for several yards before the water reached his knees. The others followed cautiously, and in a few minutes they were ashore in wild grass, growing rank and tall to their waists. They continued straight ahead for the foot of the bluffs, but instead came to another swift-flowing stream. "Confound it," Girard muttered. "We must have struck an island."

"Too swift to cross here," De Rudio said. "We'll try farther up."

They turned into a thick cluster of buffalo berries, the branches shining silvery in dim moonlight. Thorns caught at O'Neill's shirt. A startled voice, guttural and menacing, challenged out of the darkness.

Girard and Jackson wheeled their horses. "Save yourselves!" De Rudio cried, and slapped the haunch of Girard's horse. The two mounted men dashed away, splashing into the river. O'Neill dropped to his knees in the high grass. A few inches away he could hear De Rudio breathing.

A moment later a band of Indians galloped out of the clump of buffalo berry bushes in pursuit of Girard and Jackson. For awhile O'Neill remained motionless in the grass, listening to sounds of the chase. Two or three shots were fired across the stream, and then De Rudio spoke softly: "O'Neill, they've gone."

For what seemed an eternity they wandered along the eastern edge of the island, trying to find a shallows. Several times they waded out, but the channel was too deep and swift. Both of them were thoroughly soaked, and O'Neill began shivering. "Lieutenant, my boots are full of water and my clothing is dripping."

De Rudio mumbled something in Italian, pointing to the sky. It was turning gray in the east. O'Neill quickly removed his outer clothing. He shook water from his boots, dried the insides as best he could with grass, and then wrung out his socks and shirt and pants. When he put his clothing back on, he shivered again as the clammy wool touched his skin.

A clatter of hoofs sounded from across the river, and a column of mounted men began passing in front of them. De Rudio stood up, peering through the gray mists. "O'Neill I believe it's part of the regiment!"

O'Neill clutched his carbine and followed the lieutenant to the riverbank. Some of the horses were gray. Troop E's, he thought. They'd been with Custer. The leader wore a buckskin jacket, top boots and a wide-brimmed white hat. "Captain Tom Custer!" De Rudio cried excitedly. He megaphoned his hands and called: "Halloa! Tom Custer! Tom, don't leave us here!"

A second later the column halted. A war whoop sounded, and then guns flashed orange and a volley of shots was poured into the island.

O'Neill could hear the bullets—*pict, pict, pict, pict*—cutting the brush all around him. De Rudio ducked and ran for the nearest clump of buffalo berries, O'Neill at his heels. Already the dawn's light had brightened so they could see the riders were all Indians clad in 7th Cavalry uniforms and mounted on horses taken from Custer's battalion. None of the Indians made any effort to cross the swirling river. They moved on up a cut in the bluff toward Major Reno's position, stopping occasionally to fire back at the island.

"General Custer must have suffered a terrible defeat." De Rudio said gravely.

"Our chances don't look good now, do they, sir?"

"We'll try, O'Neill, we'll try." De Rudio was peering all around him. "Now that daylight is coming, we must find another hiding place. Come on." He led the way, crawling through the grass to another clump of shrubbery, and just as they rose up to circle it, seven mounted Indians appeared from nowhere.

De Rudio immediately opened fire with his pistol, and

O'Neill pulled the trigger of his carbine without raising it to his shoulder. The Indian ponies reared, plunging so that their riders could not bring guns or bows into play. Two Indians fell from their mounts, which galloped away.

"Run!" De Rudio shouted. For a hundred yards or more they ran. A single bullet screamed over their heads. There was enough light now so that they could see a jumble of driftwood which had been piled up by floods. They leaped over the logs and looked back, weapons ready. The Indians were too busy rounding up their frightened ponies to make an immediate attack.

"This is a perfect fortification," De Rudio declared cheerfully. "Logs all around us." He shook hands with O'Neill. "Your eye was true and your carbine trusty, O'Neill. If we must die, we'll die together—fighting. How is your ammunition holding up?"

O'Neill removed his cartridge belt and counted. "Twenty-five rounds, sir."

"I have twelve. That's thirty-seven dead Indians."

They both laughed in relief, cutting it off when two shots sounded suddenly from across the river. Almost immediately carbines began rattling along the bluffs. War whoops of Indians and the cheering of Reno's soldiers added to the din.

From their position among the logs, O'Neill and De Rudio could see their comrades on the heights, silhouetted against yellow morning sunlight. They seemed to be holding off the attacking wave of Indians.

A bullet shrieked and slapped into one of the logs. O'Neill sighted down his carbine barrel. A hundred yards away, Indian feathers moved above the waving grass. "Don't fire," De Rudio said. "They're not sure where we are." A few more shots spattered into the driftwood. The lieutenant shrugged. "They're trying to draw our fire. If they come into the clearing, we'll have to shoot, but wait until they're close enough to make every bullet count."

O'Neill was almost sure now he would never get off the

island alive. He wondered how he could accept this and not be afraid. He supposed it was because Lieutenant De Rudio was not afraid. He would never have guessed, back at Fort Lincoln or on the march, that such a bragging dandy as De Rudio could be so brave a man.

Far down in the high grass a wisp of smoke twirled upward. A second later flames leaped high. The crackling of burning grass sounded like distant carbine fire.

De Rudio gasped. "The devils! They're trying to burn us out!"

Fortunately there was not much wind to drive the blaze into them, but it was steadily eating its way toward the driftwood. If enough fire reached the dry debris around their crude fort, the whole would quickly be set to blazing.

New green growth under the dry sedge created billows of smoke which hung over the island. De Rudio pulled on his gauntlets. "The Indians can't see us now for certain, O'Neill, but keep me covered." He leaped over the logs and began clearing away dead limbs and leaves. When the first ring of fire came near, he beat it out with his gloved hands. In a few minutes the line of flames went past them, burning its way down the island.

De Rudio crawled back into the logs, grinning. His dark face was smudged with soot. "Well, here we are in a little oasis, more secure than before. Now the devils can't sneak up on us in the grass."

On the bluffs, another burst of firing indicated a second charge by the Indians. Again the soldiers drove their assailants away.

De Rudio wiped his face with his handkerchief. Smoke permeated the air, irritating eyes, nose and lungs. "I don't think they'll come after us now, O'Neill. But it'll be a long day.

"Yes, sir. I hope the boys on the hill can hold out."

The lieutenant nodded. "O'Neill, are you married?"

"No, sir."

"Well, I wouldn't mind this so much if I weren't. I worry about what my wife and children will do if I don't get out of here."

"I can understand that, sir." O'Neill blinked his eyes against the smoke. "I'd like to get out of here alive too. I hope to become a surgeon someday."

"A fine ambition for a young man."

"Surgeon DeWolf has promised to put my name in for hospital steward when we get back to Fort Lincoln."

"I'd be proud to add my recommendation to his, O'Neill."

"Thank you, sir."

Time dragged on. They saw no more signs of Indians on the island, but many were gathering across the river under the bluffs. About midafternoon the warriors made a massed charge, the foremost reaching the very top of the hill. For a few minutes fighting was hand to hand, but Reno's men countercharged and drove them away once again.

Late in the afternoon they saw a squad of troopers creeping down a gash in the bluffs. "They're after water," De Rudio said. Several men in the party had canteens slung over both shoulders, and some were carrying camp kettles. Their ravine cover ended about thirty feet from the river. As soon as they moved out on the bank, they would be exposed to fire.

Half the party took firing positions, then the others dashed for the river. Almost immediately, Indians above them opened fire. The men at the riverbank held their ground, coolly filling their canteens and kettles.

"Here, O'Neill, hand me your carbine!" De Rudio took the weapon, sighted and fired. An Indian toppled from his sniping position behind a chokecherry bush. De Rudio fired again.

Now the water party was hurrying back to the ravine, their comrades pouring a heavy covering fire against the Indians. One man in the water detail was hit. He went down, crawled for a few feet into the ravine, and lay there unnoticed by his withdrawing comrades. An Indian dropped down to scalp him, but De Rudio felled the attacker with a single shot.

"That leaves us thirty-four cartridges," the lieutenant said. "They may come after us now, if any of the devils noticed my fire."

For another hour they kept an unceasing vigil, alert for signs of movement on all sides of their little fort. The sun dropped behind the western hills. The musketry rattle ceased on the bluffs, and only an occasional far-off shot was heard.

About dusk a party of squaws and children passed along the west bank, moving upriver. The squaws were mounted on horses dragging travois loaded with camp equipment rolled in tepee skins. "They're breaking camp," De Rudio said.

"I haven't heard or seen any sign of our boys for more than an hour, sir."

De Rudio frowned. "They may have left the field, or Custer may have reached them. We have no way of knowing."

"What will we do if we can't find them tonight, sir? We haven't eaten for two days, and to tell you the truth, I'm beginning to feel rather weak."

"You'd be surprised how long a man can go without food, O'Neill. If we have it to do, we can make our way back to our base on the Yellowstone, traveling by night, hiding by day. We can pick up scraps in our old camps, or maybe shoot a deer or antelope."

As soon as darkness came on, they left the pile of driftwood, moved cautiously back to the shallows they had crossed to reach the island, and returned to the west bank. Several Indian campfires were burning in the valley, the nearest one about a hundred yards away. But there were no victory celebrations on this night.

They walked south for a mile or more, finally discovering a ford that was only waist deep. When they reached the other side, a dark, steep bluff rose directly before them. Nothing of life could be seen or heard, not a sound except the wind sighing through grass and sagebrush.

They wrung out their wet uniforms, crawled up the bluffs, looking and listening. "Our men must have marched away," De Rudio whispered. Except for the tiny twinkling fires they had left behind, the great valley of the Little Big Horn seemed entirely deserted.

"To keep our sense of direction," De Rudio continued, "we'd best go south, pick up our old trail, and follow it down to the Rosebud."

With the shining, twisting river on their right as a guide, they began walking at a brisk pace, occasionally stumbling over a gully or grass hummock. After a mile or so a high knoll loomed in front of them. "If our men have lighted campfires, we may be able to see them from up there," De Rudio said.

O'Neill dug his boots into the clay and began climbing. In ten minutes they were at the top. No fires were in sight anywhere.

Then out of the darkness behind them came the unmistakable bray of a mule. "One of our pack mules, sir!" O'Neill cried softly.

"Indeed it was," the lieutenant replied. "We must have gone past Major Reno's position. This crooking river is deceptive."

They turned back north again, keeping to high ground, stopping every few yards to listen. Finally after climbing a slight rise, they sighted a campfire. A few minutes later they heard voices.

"Are they our boys or not?" O'Neill whispered.

De Rudio turned his head to one side, listening. "I can't tell."

They began crawling along the ground on their stomachs,

hitching along a few inches at a time. Whether the camp was Indians or soldiers, O'Neill expected every moment to hear the explosion of a gun, the wail of a bullet. The campfire was now only two hundred yards away.

A voice drawled out of the shadows: "Bring that horse over here, Trooper."

O'Neill recognized the Irish brogue immediately, and called: "Sergeant Ryan! Don't shoot on us! It's O'Neill and Lieutenant De Rudio!"

Another voice, closer by, challenged: "Halt, who goes there?"

De Rudio answered: "Picket, don't fire! It's Lieutenant De Rudio!"

"Come on in!"

O'Neill and De Rudio sprang to their feet, and jogtrotted toward the campfire.

"De Rudio!" someone shouted, and in the dim light O'Neill recognized Lieutenant Varnum. "Am I happy to see you!" Varnum cried. "You wild I-talian! Girard and Billy Jackson told us they had to leave you, and we'd counted you out. In fact I was sleeping in your bedroll, having lost mine."

"And how I've missed it, Varnum. Haven't had a wink for two nights."

Sergeant Ryan stepped into the light, reminding O'Neill of a ghost, with his head and arm swathed in bandages. "You skinny bean pole," Ryan drawled. "Come on to the fire, O'Neill, and put some coffee and bacon in your empty carcass."

"Give him your best rations, Sergeant," De Rudio said. "Trooper O'Neill stood by me like a brother."

"Yes, sir!"

As the warmth of the fire enveloped O'Neill's chilled body, he noticed a tall man rising from a nearby blanket roll. The man rubbed his eyes and took an unsteady step or two, staring at the scene around the campfire. "For the love of Pete, can't a man *ever* get any sleep—thunderation, it's De Rudio and Trooper O'Neill!"

His face came into the firelight, his long mustaches dusty and bedraggled, his eyes hollow, a young face turned old— Lieutenant Edward Godfrey.

19

Lieutenant
Edward Godfrey

June 27–28

"I haven't had my uniform off for three days," Godfrey said. "Never felt so done up and plain dirty." He sat down wearily between De Rudio and Varnum. He winced, changed his position, and with an odd look reached into his coat pocket and removed a tin can. "So that's what I was sitting on. Forgot all about this can of California pears. I've been hoarding it against thirst and starvation."

He blinked at the fire, which blazed up when Sergeant Ryan dropped some brush upon it. "You have a sharp knife, De Rudio?"

"I lost it somewhere in the woods by the river," the Italian replied.

Varnum handed Godfrey a hunting knife, and Godfrey jabbed a hole in the can. "A great invention," he said. "Canned fruit. I hear an Italian invented it."

"No, it was a Frenchman," said De Rudio.

Godfrey offered him the opened can. "I thought the Italians discovered everything."

"We discovered America."

Godfrey and Varnum both laughed. "Our red-skinned

friends prowling out there might dispute that," Godfrey said. They passed the can around, savoring the pears and the juice.

"You've heard nothing from Custer?" De Rudio asked.

Godfrey shook his head. "Nothing."

De Rudio told him about seeing the gray horses and the warrior dressed in what appeared to be Tom Custer's clothing. "The general must've had a bad time."

"We noticed gray horses in some of the charges today," Godfrey said. "Tom Weir thinks the general is in the same fix we are. Besieged on a hill down river. Weir took his troop up to the farthest point, and claims he saw a tremendous battle going on.

"Captain Weir would have marched on and joined Custer," Varnum added, "but the Indians drove him back here."

Godfrey rested his chin on his hands, staring at the fire. "That was a nasty business. Reno wanted to court-martial Tom Weir for moving without orders, but I believe Benteen has talked him out of it. We were all skittery that first day. Today was a different story. Every man on this hill ought to have a medal for the way we fought today."

Varnum yawned and said: "I'd trade my medal to be off this hill and away from these infernal redskins."

"I'm glad to be on this hill," De Rudio told him firmly. He chewed slowly on the last of the pears. "You'd think we would have heard from Custer or Terry by now."

"I figure Custer got away," said Varnum. "He must have seen the fix we are in and skedaddled to find Terry and bring him on here in a hurry."

"Terry was supposed to be in reach of us today," Godfrey said.

Sergeant Ryan called from the fire: "Coffee boiling, gentlemen."

The three officers arose and filled tin cups generously from the camp kettle. "Thanks to the pack mules," Godfrey commented, "we're doing rather well up here for rations. And without that extra ammunition we'd all be dead men tonight. Plenty of everything but medical supplies and water."

"I saw one of your water details from the island," De Rudio said.

Sergeant Ryan spoke up: "We lost two of our best men, sir, getting that water for the wounded. Since dark, though, the boys have brought up enough to last us for awhile."

A heavy-set man emerged from the shadows, his shoulders bowed with weariness. "I'll take a cup of that brown liquid," he said hoarsely.

Godfrey stepped back, making room for him. "I'm sure you need it worse than any of us, Surgeon."

Dr. Porter pushed his walrus mustaches back with one finger and took a deep swallow. "Ah, Lieutenant De Rudio," he said. "I heard you made it back safely to us. I'm thankful I don't have to add you to my already overcrowded hospital."

De Rudio bowed slightly. "How many do you have, sir?"

"Fifty-one."

The Italian whistled softly. "That leaves us with only about two hundred for duty."

"Less than that. We've also counted at least fifty dead or missing. And if I don't get medical supplies soon, a goodly number of my wounded will join them."

De Rudio shook his head. "Not two hundred troopers left. And against some thousands of Indians."

"I figured three thousand warriors around us yesterday," Varnum said.

The surgeon reached in his pocket and held a handful of bullets into the firelight. "These don't bode too well for our friends with Custer. I took them out of our wounded today. Forty-fives. To my eye they are military issue."

"Captured from Custer's men you think?" Godfrey asked.

"Some from our own losses across the river perhaps, but the odds point to considerably more carbines and cartridges taken from somewhere else."

Godfrey downed the last of his coffee, and refilled his cup from the kettle. "Well, they *felt* our fire today, or yesterday I suppose it is now. They may not have the stomach for another taste of it." He managed a feeble chuckle. "I'll never forget Captain French up there on his line, sitting cross-legged like a tailor, bellowing his firing orders."

"Begging the lieutenant's pardon," Ryan put in, "I'd like to say there was never a braver captain in the 7th Regiment than the captain you speak of, my Captain French. Why, when we rushed down this noon to help Captain Benteen's troop out of a fix they'd got in, Captain French mounted that gray horse of his and charged right in a bunch of redskins, trampling them down. When an Indian shot his horse under him, the captain just stepped out of the saddle as cool as custard and covered the rest of us in a withdrawal to our pits."

"He's rawhide, all the way through," Godfrey agreed.

Boots scraped on the hard ground, and Captain Benteen strode into the firelight. His white hair was tousled. "Coffee-coolers to a man," he greeted them sourly. "The whole lot of you look like a bunch of trading-post Indians."

"You could do with a fresh press in your pants, too, Captain," Dr. Porter replied. "What brings you out of your blanket roll? You swore to me you were going to round up some sleep tonight."

"Tonight it's too quiet," Benteen complained. He dipped himself a cup of coffee. "Last night it was too noisy." He squinted at De Rudio. "So you made it in, Lieutenant? Well, you should've been here last night. Some redskin plumped me in the heel of my boot while I was trying to gather a few winks. Another bullet scattered the dry dust under my armpit. However, I hadn't the remotest idea of letting little things like that disturb me, when a sergeant came clattering up and told me my troop was having a regular monkey-and-parrot time of it. It was to and fro from then till daylight, and then the show really started." He looked off to the east where the sky was beginning to lighten. "No, gentlemen, it's just *too* quiet for a man to sleep tonight."

"How is the major?" Porter asked.

"He finally dozed off."

"You think he's going to be all right?" Godfrey asked softly.

Benteen began filling his pipe. "Reno? Nothing wrong with Reno. If you'd lived through what he did in the war—well, that was ten years ago, but Reno knows he should have been killed a dozen times . . ." Benteen plucked a coal from the fire and dropped it in his pipe bowl. "If we get out of this scrape, there's going to be a lot of wild talk about Reno, no way of stopping it. Just put yourself in his place, that's all. What would you have done if you'd been in command, I ask you?"

Nobody spoke. Godfrey thought to himself: All I know is I'm glad Fred Benteen was on this hill yesterday.

Streaks of violet and rose stained the sky, and shapes of men and horses materialized in the grayness of dawn. Sounds echoed hollowly—footsteps, groans, the rattle of harness metal. Across these undertones, a bugle sounded reveille.

With a sigh, Dr. Porter raised himself. "Another day," he said.

"For all of us." Benteen tossed coffee grounds into the fire. "Ready Godfrey?"

A horseman cantered up. Recognizing Major Reno, they all arose. "Stay as you are, gentlemen." Reno dismounted and took the cup of coffee offered him by Sergeant Ryan. He had slicked his hair down with water, and seemed relaxed and in full command of himself. "I've just made a circuit of our lines," he said. "The men report a quiet night. Absolutely no signs of hostiles."

"It's entirely too quiet to my mind," Benteen drawled.

Reno nodded to De Rudio. "Welcome back, Lieutenant."

"I'm glad to be here, sir. For what it's worth, late last evening I saw quite a large party of squaws moving south along the other side of the river."

"Yes, I observed them also."

"No warriors with them," Benteen said. "Sitting Bull's scouts may have brought in news of Terry's column, and so he cleared the squaws out before another big fight."

Reno swung back into his saddle. "We'll soon know. Be ready for a trick."

Benteen pulled his big hat over his mop of hair. "They like to attack at dawn. Let's get to our positions, gentlemen."

"Where's A Troop?" De Rudio asked.

"Moylan's defending on my far right," Godfrey told him. "Just walk toward that rising sun. He'll be glad to see you."

Hurrying on to the north point of the ridge, Godfrey scanned the slopes and valleys to right and left for any signs of movement. At every moment he expected to hear war whoops signaling the beginning of another day of siege.

When he reached the K Troop rifle pits, a sergeant saluted him. "All quiet, sir."

"No 'morning gun' from the Sioux, eh, Sergeant?"

"No, sir, and take a look down there where the village was."

Godfrey stared across the tree-fringed river. Where gray-coned tepees had been the day before, now were only pole scaffolds standing like skeletons in the first light of morning. "They've moved out, Sergeant. At least the squaws and children have." He glanced along the K Troop defense position. "See that the men are all wide awake. I think I'll have a word with Captain French."

Godfrey crossed the narrow point to M Troop's pits and found Captain French hunkered down in the center of his line, gnawing on a piece of hardtack and frowning at the river valley. "Not an Indian in sight, Godfrey. What do you think?"

Godfrey chuckled. "I came over here to ask you that same question. Either they've left us, or they're going to try something very tricky."

"Reno fears a trap," French said.

"He may be right."

A detail of men headed by Sergeant Ryan came walking slowly from the field hospital. They were carrying two forms wrapped in gray blankets.

"Burial party," French said solemnly. "Troopers Tanner and Voight. They got it in that charge yesterday."

Godfrey stood to one side while French supervised the hasty burial of the two M Troop men. During the night a double grave had been dug in the hard gray earth. No one could find a Bible, but the captain remembered a verse and recited it slowly in his deep voice: "We are strangers before thee, and sojourners, as were all our fathers. Our days on the earth are as a shadow, and there is none abiding. Amen."

To conserve ammunition, no volleys were fired over the grave. At a signal from Sergeant Ryan, the men spaded in the dirt, mounding it up. Then the sergeant stepped forward with a board taken from a hardtack box. Written upon it with a lead pencil were the names of the dead. Ryan drove this crude marker into the ground at the head of the grave.

"Thank you, Sergeant," French said. He was gazing off at the northeastern horizon. "Godfrey, what do you make of that cloud dust off yonder?"

Godfrey fixed his field glass on a yellow smudge against the sky line. "Eight or ten miles out," he said. "That could be our Indians. Coming or going?"

"It wasn't there ten minutes ago," French replied. "We'd better inform Major Reno."

They found Reno in the hospital area. The major studied the dust carefully through the glass. "Wind is blowing the stuff our way so I can't make out whether the horsemen are wearing blue uniforms or not. Have Trumpeter Martin sound assembly."

As the officers gathered, each one was asked to examine the dust cloud. "My guess is it's one of our columns," Benteen said. "Custer, Terry, maybe Crook. But my old eyes can't be sure, so I say we'd better collect our horses, fill all our camp kettles and canteens from the river, and be ready for a worse day than yesterday."

For an hour the troopers on the hill remained in suspense; then the horsemen were close enough to recognize as soldiers. "No gray horse troop in the column," Reno said. "So it can't be Custer."

"Unless Custer lost his gray horse troop," said Captain Weir.

"I can't believe that." Reno blinked his eyes against the sun. "Crook wouldn't be coming from the northeast, so it must be Terry or Gibbon. We'll send out scouts to meet them."

"That won't be necessary, sir," Godfrey said, pointing down the slope. "A horseman coming there. In buckskins. Must be from the column."

In a few minutes every trooper on the hill was watching the galloping rider. A spontaneous cheer broke from the rifle pits.

"It's Muggins Taylor," Varnum declared. "One of General Gibbon's scouts."

Taylor approached slowly. His horse was tired from the fast run and the climb up the hill. "I'm looking for General Custer," he called out.

Reno stepped forward. "I am in command here. We do not know where the general is."

The scout dismounted and removed a folded note from his gauntlet. "It's addressed to Custer, but General Terry told me to deliver it to the first officer I found."

Reno took the message and read it hurriedly. His expression was grave when he looked up at his officers. "Terry says he met two Crow scouts from Custer's battalion. They told him our regiment had been whipped and nearly all killed. Terry says he does not believe their story, but is advancing in a forced march with medical assistance."

Captain Weir spoke, his voice bitter: "I believe the Crows' story. And it's a little late for medical assistance for General Custer's men, I fear."

Reno compressed his lips, frowning at Weir. "I dare say we'll find the general as well off as we are."

"I hope so," Weir replied.

Godfrey glanced at the dust cloud, now no more than three miles away. Off to the north he noticed a small band of horsemen trotting along the ridge tops. "That must be some of Custer's men coming there," he cried excitedly.

The riders were not Custer's men, nor were they cavalrymen. They were a mounted detail of infantry, scouting ahead of Terry's column. To Godfrey's surprise, the officer in command was an old friend, Lieutenant James Bradley.

"Jim Bradley!" Godfrey greeted him. "You've come from down river. Did you see any signs of Custer?" Godfrey offered his hand to assist Bradley in dismounting. Reno and the other officers gathered around.

Bradley's face was grim. "Ed, I'm afraid General Custer and his men are done for."

"What do you base this on, Lieutenant?" Reno demanded.

"Observation," Bradley replied. "Through my field glass I counted a hundred and ninety-seven dead bodies.

"You did not march over the battlefield?"

"No, sir. As you see, I have only a small force, and Indians have been on my flanks since I left the column. When I sighted your flag, I turned this way."

In less than an hour the column came into plain view on the west side of the river. Terry had crossed at one of the fords into the abandoned Indian village, and now the main body was halting in the valley just below the bluffs. Gatling guns were already moving into defensive positions, and Godfrey could not help recalling Custer's decision to cut them loose from the regiment. What a difference the battery of Gatlings would have made, he thought.

Through his field glass, Godfrey saw General Terry talking with General Gibbon. Suddenly Terry wheeled his horse and started across the river. "General Terry is coming up, sir!" he called to Reno.

"Yes, I'm sending Lieutenants Hare and Wallace down to escort him."

All along the ridge, the troopers came out of their rifle pits and began waving their hats and cheering. By the time Terry had reached the first outposts, the reception had become tumultuous.

But when Terry came close enough for the men to see his face, the cheers died away, and then there was a frozen silence. General Terry was weeping.

Godfrey hurried forward with Reno and the other officers, to meet him. Reno saluted and called a greeting. Terry held up his hand, his voice strangling at first as he tried to speak. "I have seen where Custer died," he said. "The flower of the Army is gone at last."

Terry's first concern was for the wounded. He was distressed when he saw fifty men lying in the open with only one surgeon to attend them. "We must get these wounded down to Gibbons' camp. Major Reno, assign details from each of your troops to fashion hand litters from blankets, shirts, anything—and start moving your wounded off this bluff."

Reno passed the order to the troop commanders, and Godfrey hastened to put his men to work. Other orders followed rapidly. Arms and equipment which had been scattered during the fighting were collected. All articles not claimed were assumed to belong to the dead or wounded. As it was impossible to transport extra gear, everything left over was tossed into a blazing fire—saddles, bridles, damaged carbines.

Late in the day Godfrey led his troop down to Gibbons' camp with the last of the litter-bearers. There he learned that detachments sent out to search for survivors of Custer's battalion had all returned. They had found only dead men. He also received orders from Benteen to be ready to march to the Custer battlefield at daylight. A detachment of the most able survivors of the 7th Regiment had been assigned the task of burying their comrades who had fallen with Custer.

The next morning was a beautiful one, with birds singing again in the trees along the Little Big Horn. The men marched without their usual bantering remarks, their progress marked only by muffled beats of hoofs in sand, the creak of leather, the snorting of horses, the rattle of spades and shovels.

Following the well-beaten trail where thousands of Indian ponies had galloped a few hours before, they marched past ghostly skeletons of tepees. At the first ford, Benteen signaled the column to turn right. They splashed across the river and climbed a hill.

When they reached the summit, Benteen wheeled to the left and ordered a halt. Godfrey trotted his horse forward, overtaking Captain Weir, and the two rode together to the advance position. Benteen was standing in his stirrups, staring off across the rolling landscape.

"What are those?" Weir exclaimed.

The greenish-brown slopes were dotted with dead horses and objects which appeared to be white boulders. Godfrey's fingers trembled as he held up his field glass. "The dead!" he answered hoarsely.

"How white they look!" Weir said. "How white!"

"Stripped of everything," Benteen whispered. "Arms, ammunition, equipment, clothing." His breath came out in a deep sigh. "Let's get on with it." He raised his hand, and the column moved on to the silent battlefield.

They found Captain Keogh lying untouched within a ring of dead horses. His shirt had been removed. His Agnus Dei medal lay on his chest, shining in the morning sunlight. They found General Custer on the highest point, with dozens of slain horses and a full troop of dead around him. The only marks upon him were bullet wounds in his temple and chest. He looked as if he had fallen asleep. "You could almost imagine him standing before you," Benteen said solemnly.

All morning they worked, digging with spades, axes, picks and hatchets. In the afternoon, Benteen ordered Godfrey to take a small mounted detail and make a complete circle of the outer fringes of the battlefield. They were to search for any bodies which might be hidden in gullies or high grass.

Godfrey ended this melancholy circuit at the banks of the river. It was shady there, and he told his men to dismount and rest for a few minutes after their long, slow march under the hot sun.

He felt gloomy and very tired. He sat down and tried to collect his thoughts. The day had seemed unreal, like a sorrowful dream.

His eyelids drooped. Off in the distance he could hear sounds of picks and shovels striking hard earth. When he opened his eyes again, he saw something moving in the brush along the riverbank. It was a horse, a clay-colored horse, walking very painfully and slowly—Captain Keogh's horse Comanche.

20

Comanche

June 28, 1876–April 10, 1878

Comanche neighed, very faintly. Trooper Gustave Korn, who was in Lieutenant Godfrey's detail, stood up and called the horse's name. He and two or three of the men began walking toward him.

Trooper Korn was surprised that the Indians had overlooked so fine a horse as Comanche. When he came nearer, he thought he understood why. The animal was badly hurt. Crimson stains blotched flanks and legs. Blood oozed from a deep neck wound. Captain Keogh's saddle hung under Comanche's belly. The bridle was broken, the bit dangling. The proud animal raised his head then let it droop wearily.

"Shoot him," a trooper said. "Put him out of his misery."

"No!" cried Korn. "This is Captain Keogh's horse. I'll take care of him." He glanced imploringly at Lieutenant Godfrey. "We can't destroy Comanche, can we, sir?"

"The horse appears to be about done for, Korn," Godfrey replied."

"I'm a blacksmith, sir, and I know a deal about horses. He looks to me as if he had the spirit to live. Captain Keogh was my captain. Had I not been with the pack mules, I'd have died with him. I *know* the captain would want us to try and save Comanche."

Godfrey moved in closer, shaking his head as he examined the wounds. At the same time, Sergeant Henry Brinkerhoff unloosed the saddle and tossed it aside. "He's lived two days already, Lieutenant," Brinkerhoff said. "Couldn't we give him one more day? I'll help Korn wash his wounds and get him back to camp."

"We'll all help," another trooper said.

Godfrey shrugged. "I suppose it's worth a try. Comanche *is* the only survivor. All right, Korn, you and the sergeant do what you can."

Korn knotted the broken bridle together, and he and Brinkerhoff led the horse slowly toward the ford, most of the other troopers following.

"Hold up, the rest of you," Godfrey called harshly. "There's still work to do on the hill. Mount up."

Darkness was falling when Comanche limped into camp escorted by Gustave Korn, Sergeant Brinkerhoff and several other troopers who had done without their suppers to volunteer for the mission. By the time they arrived, the entire camp had heard about the miracle of Comanche's survival. A great bed of dried grass had been collected, and as Comanche was half led, half carried to this resting place, the men lined up and cheered.

Weary as they were after attending fifty wounded men all day, Dr. Porter and the surgeons with Gibbon's column offered their services. Comanche lay quietly while the surgeons examined him. "Ten wounds I count," Dr. Porter said. "Three bad ones—neck, lung and groin. I've seen worse wounded men who lived. But it'll be a miracle."

"It's already been a miracle, sir," Trooper Korn declared.

"This horse needs nourishment as well as medication," Dr. Paulding said. "What do you suggest, Porter?"

"Corn-meal mash."

"With brandy," Paulding added. "I have the better part of a bottle of Hennesy. Count it contributed to the cause."

Porter began applying salve to the wounds. "This column marches tomorrow with our wounded men for the *Far West*. To the mouth of the Little Big Horn. We can never move a wounded horse that far, you know, Korn."

"We'll get him there," Korn replied, "if I have to carry him on my back." He glanced around, was surprised to see General Terry standing behind him, and saluted quickly.

Terry returned the salute and said: "Saving that horse seems to have become an obsession of the entire command." His eyes twinkled. "Do you think he could be floated down to the Big Horn on a raft, Trooper?"

Korn's face brightened. "Yes, sir, we could try that. I'm sure the boys will pitch in and help me build one. We can do it tonight."

"Wait until tomorrow," the general said. "I had a detail put a strong log raft together this afternoon. They'll try it out as soon as daylight comes. If it'll move down this crooked stream, I intend to have more built to float our wounded men to the *Far West*."

When taps sounded, Gustave Korn put his blanket roll near Comanche's grass bed. Neither trooper nor the horse slept very much that night. Comanche was restless, and every time Korn heard him moving about, he would rise and try to spoon more of the brandy mash down the animal's throat.

Soon after reveille, a platoon boarded the log raft and shoved off for a trial run. Terry ordered units formed for a march alongside the river. As three men were required for each of the hand litters, almost every able-bodied soldier was assigned to carry the wounded. Trooper Korn and a volunteer detail with Comanche brought up the rear with the horse and mule herds.

Their destination—the mouth of the Little Big Horn—lay 22 miles to the north. Six hours later, when they stopped for nooning, the litter bearers had marched only 3 miles. Terry halted at the shallow ford below the Custer battlefield, and he and his staff turned back to learn what had happened to the raft. It had been blocked by driftwood, and the lieutenant in command was having no success in breaking a way through.

"We'll have to try something else," Terry declared. "Mule litters."

"We have plenty of mules, sir," his adjutant said, "but no nails or rope."

"We'll use the Indians' substitutes for nails and rope," Terry replied crisply. "Rawhide. There are more than enough dead horses around here to supply our needs."

"Yes, sir."

"I want every available man in the command put to cutting poles and skinning horses. The skinning won't be pleasant, but it must be done."

Into the late afternoon the soldiers labored over construction of mule litters. Ten men had recovered sufficiently to ride in saddles again, leaving forty-two requiring litter transportation.

To build each litter, two poles 3 inches in diameter and 13 feet long were laid side by side, 3 feet apart. Then two short pieces were laid 7 feet apart across the poles and bound to them with rawhide. Next a network of rawhide was woven from one pole to another. Two loops at the ends, reaching like bows from pole to pole, completed the frame. A bed and pillow of grass, covered with a blanket, completed the litter. A mule was then backed into the front end between the poles which served as shafts, and the rawhide loop was placed over its pack saddle. Another mule was led into the rear end of the poles, with its head facing toward the front mule's tail, and the loop of rawhide placed over its pack saddle.

By late afternoon the forty-two litters were finished. General Terry and Dr. Porter inspected each one and pronounced them ready for service. When some of the wounded men expressed fear of being jolted, Porter reassured them. "Like riding on a cloud, boys. The springy green side poles and the give in the rawhide will smooth out all the bumps. Just lie there and sleep like kings. Wouldn't mind being invalided myself."

Gustave Korn, meanwhile, had not been idle. He and Sergeant Brinkerhoff secured several wide strips of horsehide and fastened them to two parallel poles. They knew that when the column resumed march it would move much faster than before. To keep Comanche going, they would use four to six men on each side pole, with the rawhide bands running under his belly to partially support him.

As sunset was still three hours away, Terry decided to resume march until dark. Progress was so rapid that when night fell he decided to push on.

Comanche was growing weaker, but Korn had no trouble finding volunteers to take turns shouldering the long poles. Every man in the 7th Cavalry was determined that Comanche would get to the *Far West.*

For a while the moon lighted the trail, but clouds began gathering before midnight and then blackness closed down. Cavalrymen and infantrymen became jumbled up. They shouted angrily at one another. Mules stumbled, and the wounded cried out in pain or alarm.

The last half of the march was up and down hills and through beds of tall cactus which could not be seen in time to avoid. Korn almost gave up while crossing a thick growth of these dreaded plants which slapped at legs like evil, living things, leaving needles which burned piercingly. Some of Comanche's wounds reopened, and the animal had no strength left at all.

Then a slow chill rain began falling. When the men unrolled their ponchos, Korn demanded that they be given up to be placed over Comanche.

The last mile down to the *Far West* was the worst. Clay

had turned to a slick muck under the rain, and the men with Comanche fell behind the column. Korn suddenly realized that they were lost. "Brinkerhoff, where is the column?"

The sergeant was breathing hard. "I think they've lost us, Gustave. Wait a minute! Look there!"

Far down the slope, a blaze glimmered through the drizzle. Then another and another. "They're lighting flares," Brinkerhoff said.

Along both sides of a ravine, brush fires burned brightly, and they could see the column winding down toward the *Far West.*

After another hour of hard work, they brought Comanche to the side of the river steamer. Without the support of the five men on either side of him, the horse could not have stood erect.

Captain Grant Marsh and General Terry came tramping down the wide gangplank. "Is he still alive?" Terry asked anxiously.

"Yes, sir," Korn replied. He shifted the pole which was pressing into his weary shoulder.

"Bring him aboard," said Captain Marsh. "I've ordered my crew to prepare a special stall in the stern. They're bedding it with straw."

On July 5, the *Far West* docked at the landing in Bismarck and unloaded the wounded. Comanche was still weak, but was able to walk down the landing plank into an army wagon. The wagon pulled aboard the Fort Lincoln ferry, and a short time later he was in a clean stall and under the care of post veterinarians.

Trooper Gustave Korn was assigned the duty of watching over Comanche. For more than a year the horse was an invalid, spending much of his time suspended by a band sling. But he had become world famous and had many visitors, all eager to pay their respects to the only survivor of Custer's last battle.

Finally, in the spring of 1878, veterinarians pronounced

him fit for duty. Comanche was turned loose to graze and frolic with other horses of the 7th Cavalry.

The question naturally arose as to who would ride this most famous of all living horses. Trooper Gustave Korn? Korn expressed the hope that no one would ever ride Captain Keogh's horse. But would this be within regulations? No member of the 7th Cavalry, man or horse, had the right to remain in the regiment with no duties.

On April 10, 1878, the regimental commander settled the matter by commissioning Comanche "second commanding officer" of the 7th Cavalry. And so that there would be no misunderstanding of Comanche's rights and privileges, the regiment was assembled, and General Order No. 7 was read to each troop:

1. The horse known as Comanche, being the only living representative of the bloody tragedy of the Little Big Horn, Mont., June 25, 1876, his kind treatment and comfort should be a matter of special pride and solicitude on the part of the 7th Cavalry, to the end that his life may be prolonged to the utmost limit. Though wounded and scarred, his very silence speaks in terms more eloquent than words of the desperate struggle against overwhelming numbers of the hopeless conflict, and heroic manner in which all went down that day.

2. The commanding officer of I Troop will see that a special and comfortable stall is fitted up for Comanche; he will not be ridden by any person whatever under any circumstances, nor will he be put to any kind of work.

3. Hereafter upon all occasions of ceremony [of mounted regimental formation,] Comanche, saddled bridled, draped in mourning, and led by a mounted trooper of Troop I, will be paraded with the regiment.

About the Author

Dee Brown is the author of several western novels and a number of nonfiction books on various phases of nineteenth-century Americana. His works include *Grierson's Raid, Creek Mary's Blood, Hear the Lonesome Whistle Blow,* and *Bury My Heart at Wounded Knee.* Born in Louisiana, Dee Brown entered the world of literature as a printer.

He now lives with his wife, Sally, in Little Rock, Arkansas.

Special Offer
Buy a Dell Book
For only 50¢.

Now you can have Dell's Readers Service Listing filled with hundreds of titles. Plus, take advantage of our unique and exciting bonus book offer which gives you the opportunity to purchase a Dell book for *only 50¢*. Here's how!

Just order any five books at the regular price. Then choose any other single book listed (up to $5.95 value) for just 50¢. Use the coupon below to send for Dell's Readers Service Listing of titles today!

DELL READERS SERVICE LISTING
P.O. Box 1045, South Holland, IL. 60473

Ms./Mrs./Mr. _____

Address _____

City/State _____ Zip _____

DFCA -10/88